B8

ON BEING A MANAGER

Prepared for the B800 Course Team by Rob Paton
and updated by Sheila Cameron and Diane Preston

Foundations of Senior Management

The Open University
BUSINESS SCHOOL

COURSE TEAM

Authoring team

Rob Paton, Course Team Chair and
   Co-Chair, People Block
Greg Clark, Co-Chair, People Block
Richard Wheatcroft, Chair, Finance Block
Geoff Jones, Chair, Marketing Block
Jenny Lewis, Chair, Organizations Block
Patricia McCarthy, Course Manager
Wendy Crane, Course Manager

External contributors

Professor Stephen Watson, External
   Assessor
Professor Martin Hilb, European Adviser
Josep Artola Ortiz
George Bell
Indira Biswas-Benbow
Ann Caro
Brian Cartwright
Luis Fernando Conde Berne
Nelarine Cornelius
Nicolas Cudre-Maroux
Michael Dempsey
Nancy Finley
John Laxton
Michael Lovitt
Ohanes Missirillian
Tim Nightingale
Virginia Novarra
Maggie Parker
Serge Rosenberg
Peter Russell
Eberhard Schaumann
Tom Scott
Adam Spielman
David Stewart
Tom Walls
Barbara Waters

Production team

Linda Smith, Project Control
Helen Thompson, Software Quality Assurance
Colin Thomas, Software Design
Laury Melton, Computer Conferencing
Jenny Edwards, Product Quality Assistant
Richard Mole, Director of Production (OUBS)
Val O'Connor, Course Team Assistant
Sally Baker, Liaison Librarian
Amanda Smith, Editor
Mark Goodwin, Editor
Ruth Drage, Graphic Designer
Roy Lawrance, Graphic Artist
Doreen Tucker, Compositor
Tina Cogdell, Print Production Co-ordinator
Jan Bright, BBC Series Producer
Natasha Soma, BBC Series Production Assistant

Other contributors

Jon Billsberry
Sheila Cameron
Professor Leslie de Chernatony
Tim Clark
Chris Cornforth
Kevin Daniels
Charles Edwards
Graham Francis
Jan Gadella
Jacky Holloway
Aude Leonetti
Chris Mabey
Geoff Mallory
David Mercer
John Moss-Jones
Sue Pearce
Diane Preston
Paul Quintas
Gilly Salmon
Clare Spencer
Rosie Thomson
Amanda Waring
Jane Whiting

This text draws on material from the following Open University courses: T245 *Managing in Organizations*, B751 *Managing Development and Change* and B789 *Managing Voluntary and Non-Profit Enterprises*.

The Open University
Walton Hall, Milton Keynes MK7 6AA

First published 1995. Second edition 1996. Third edition 1999. Fourth edition 2000.
Reprinted 2000

Copyright © 2000 The Open University

Edited, designed and typeset by The Open University.

Printed in the United Kingdom by Thanet Press Ltd, Margate, Kent.

ISBN 0 7492 9720 4

For further information on Open University Business School short courses and the Certificate, Diploma and MBA programmes, please contact the Customer Service Department, The Open University, PO Box 481, Walton Hall, Milton Keynes MK7 6BN (Telephone: 01908 653473).

12163B/b800b1i4.2

CONTENTS

INTRODUCTION TO BOOK 1

This book is about what it means to manage and be a manager. It is about the common threads that tie together the tremendously varied experiences of people who get things done through others. Its aim is to help you to make sense of those experiences, to let you stand back and consider the ways in which you approach different managerial activities and the assumptions you make about your management roles. It is also about the demands that may be made on you in the future, and the knowledge, skills and understanding that a professional manager is expected to possess.

This book is both an orientation to the course and part of the course. Its aims are to:

- Prepare you for the course by introducing some of the issues involved, and by considering how the course relates to your work as a manager.

- Present substantive ideas and frameworks that will illuminate some of the challenges you face and provide new ways of thinking about familiar dilemmas.

The book starts by asking 'What is management?', and the first four sessions explore different ways of answering this question. Each answer highlights important dimensions of management but none provides the whole truth. Session 5 draws these discussions together by considering what it means to be 'good' at managing – that is, the understanding, skills and behaviour that effective managers display. Finally, Session 6 looks at how those skills and understanding develop and can be developed further; it is about how this course can extend and accelerate the incidental management learning that you engage in anyway in the course of your work, whether you are aware of it or not.

So, although this book is wide-ranging and sometimes complicated (as is its subject matter), the underlying 'story' is simple: first, a mapping of the different demands on managers and of the ways in which they contribute to their organizations; then, a consideration of the expertise required; and finally, a discussion of how this course can help to develop such expertise.

One theme runs through the book: the contrast between the way management is supposed to be – its aspirations, its public face, its rhetoric and pretensions – and the 'messy' realities of managerial work – its private face, often confused and of uncertain effectiveness. I believe we stand a better chance of living up to the aspirations if we are prepared to accept and take seriously the realities.

THE FUNCTIONS OF MANAGEMENT

Contents

1.1 Introduction

ACTIVITY 1.1

Complete the following sentence: 'An organization is ...'

Your completed sentence should not be more than about 30 words long, and should either define an organization or sum up the main distinctive qualities of organizations. When you have done this, read on.

I gave this task to a dozen managers, and they came up with answers such as: 'An organization is a body that pursues particular aims through a structure that establishes the various activities involved'; and 'An organization is a group of people working together for common aims – the work is divided up, carried out and co-ordinated to plans and rules'. Taken together, it was striking that *every one of them* produced an answer that either emphasized or hinted at *each* of the following three points.

1   The idea that the members of an organization form an identifiable, coherent whole as a result of their mutual interdependence in working on different aspects of a common task. Organizations are unified or integrated entities.

2   The idea that organizations embody a conscious design, that their structures reflect sound *means* to achieve organizational *ends*. Or, in other words, that organizations *apply knowledge about cause–effect relationships* in the use of human, financial and technological resources. In short, the idea that organizations are *rational*.

3   The idea that organizations exist to pursue particular aims and objectives. Indeed, this is the fundamental idea, because it is these aims that give the organization its structure and coherence and explain its activities. Organizations are *goal-seeking*.

Together, these ideas express a view of organizations as rational, coherent, goal-seeking entities. Even if your own answer was somewhat different or did not capture all these aspects, I am still confident that you will have immediately recognized this view as familiar and widely shared. So much so, in fact, that you may not think of it as a *view* of organizations but as *how they actually are*. Even if you do not go that far, you will probably readily concede that these assumptions describe the way organizations are *supposed* to be. That is, we take it for granted that organizations should be rational and coherent – even if they inevitably fall somewhat short of this ideal in practice.

This view of organizations is associated with an equally pervasive view of management. Put simply, management is the brain of the organization – its function is to ensure that organizations are coherent, rational and goal-seeking, and to keep them that way. This session sets out this *functional* view of management, showing how it shapes, underpins and permeates so much of what managers do – and so much of what management courses teach. However, this functional view is also problematic, and is certainly not as reassuring or as straightforward as it appears. Central tenets of this view are now strongly contested on the grounds that organizations, and managers' roles within them, have been changing in important ways. Another, perhaps more fundamental, issue concerns the difficulties of judging whether particular arrangements work as they are supposed to do. Are we, as managers, as shrewdly rational as we like to think we are?

The aims of this session are to:

- Explain the conventional, functional view of management and demonstrate its pervasive impact on organizational structure and practice.

- Highlight ways in which the conventional view is problematic and potentially misleading.

1.2 The classical view

The classic statement of the functional view was made by a Frenchman, Henri Fayol, in 1916. His thinking is summarized in Box 1.1 and, whatever else you may say about it, this definition has survived over 80 years of critical discussion. Indeed, derivatives and variants of this approach are still common – as we shall see later in this book.

Box 1.1   Fayol's definition of management

What is management? Is it anything that can be identified and can stand on its own, or is it a word, a label, that has no substance?

Fayol's answer was unique at the time. The core of his contribution is his definition of management as comprising five elements

1   To forecast and plan (in French, *prévoyance*): 'examining the future and drawing up the plan of action'.

2   To organize: 'building up the structure, material and human, of the undertaking'.

3   To command: 'maintaining activity among the personnel'.

4   To co-ordinate: 'binding together, unifying and harmonising all activity and effort'.

5   To control: 'seeing that everything occurs in conformity with established rule and expressed command'.

(Source: Pugh and Hickson, 1989, p. 86)

ACTIVITY 1.2

Spend 5 to 10 minutes considering to what extent the managerial activities listed in your Activity Log are covered by Fayol's five-part definition of management.

(a) Are there any elements that you do *not* undertake?

(b) Give examples of your activities under as many of the five headings as you can.

(c) Which of your managerial activities are not easily placed within Fayol's scheme?

You will have to decide for yourself how illuminating you find Fayol's definition. Many people have found that it gives them a useful framework for thinking about their managerial activity – an overview of what it is they are doing through all their meetings and paperwork. Others feel that it fails to highlight some of the crucial elements of managing. For example, the planning function seems to cover rather a lot, including the absolutely central activities of setting goals and making decisions. So some derivative definitions of management list one or both of these activities separately. A more far-reaching criticism is that, although one can, at a stretch, group one's managerial activities under these headings, they somehow misrepresent many of those activities. Or else one simply ends up putting them all under the 'co-ordinates' heading. There is more on this in the next section.

This view of management, like the view of organizations just noted, is essentially rational. Indeed, from this viewpoint, many – perhaps most – management practices and techniques simply involve the application of rational methods of planning, decision-making and control to one situation after another. These three core activities are familiar and easily understood in general terms, even if their application in particular circumstances is often extremely challenging.

Rational in this context means using a systematic analysis of the facts to make the best decision, rather than using a more impressionistic or intuitive approach concerned with finding an acceptable decision.

Planning

The overall goal of the organization will usually be determined for managers by other people. But managers must think about how the task given can be divided up between those involved in such a way that the various activities will fit together to achieve the desired results. The underlying logic is to devise a hierarchy of objectives – see Figure 1.1 – in order to ensure a consistency of purposes both across the organization and between immediate and underlying (longer-term) purposes.

There are no agreed conventions among managers and management writers for the use of the terms 'goal' and 'objective'. Some use objective to mean the higher level purpose and goal to refer to more specific purposes. Others simply use the terms interchangeably. Figure 1.1 shows how the terms are used in this course.

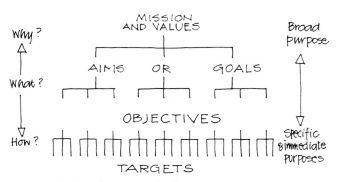

Figure 1.1 *The pyramid of purposes*

Plans usually involve three components:

- The objectives to be achieved, in terms sufficiently detailed and precise to enable others to check whether they have been achieved.

- A specification of the activities needed to achieve the objectives, with a clear understanding of how those activities relate to each other.

- Estimates of the resources needed to implement those activities, and a schedule or statement of who is to do what, with what and by when.

It is often said that objectives should be SMART: Specific, Measurable, Achievable, Relevant and Timely.

It is sometimes suggested that the components are developed in this order: first, you decide on your objectives, then you decide on how they will be achieved, and then you work out the resource implications. This is often impossible, however, because objectives, activities and resources are all *interdependent*.

Objectives have to be feasible as well as desirable, so you cannot determine them without appreciating the costs involved. However, you cannot determine costs without deciding *what* is being costed – which means knowing what the activities will be. But you cannot specify the activities without knowing the objectives they are meant to achieve ...

This means that planning does involve some 'going round in circles' as you explore different combinations of objectives, activities and resources to find the most promising way forward. A kinder way of putting this is to say that planning is an *iterative* process. It involves successive 'passes', which progressively clarify the objectives, firm up the nature and range of activities required, and determine the financial and other resources that will be needed. Inevitably, time will be spent examining options that are later discarded or trying to devise ways of achieving objectives that are modified later in the planning process. This process is represented in Figure 1.2. What starts as a general idea gradually takes shape in terms of objectives, activities and resources, which in turn are resolved into specific targets, a schedule of the tasks, budgets, staffing, and so on.

However confused the planning process may be on occasions, two things are clear: it is essentially a rational process (it involves estimation, calculation and reasoning – it results in proposals for complex chains of activity); and it is hugely important for organizations. Much management teaching concerns planning activities and tools of one kind or another – from developing a mission statement and setting objectives to forecasting techniques and the use of specialized project planning software. You will meet some of these techniques in this course.

Failing to plan is planning to fail

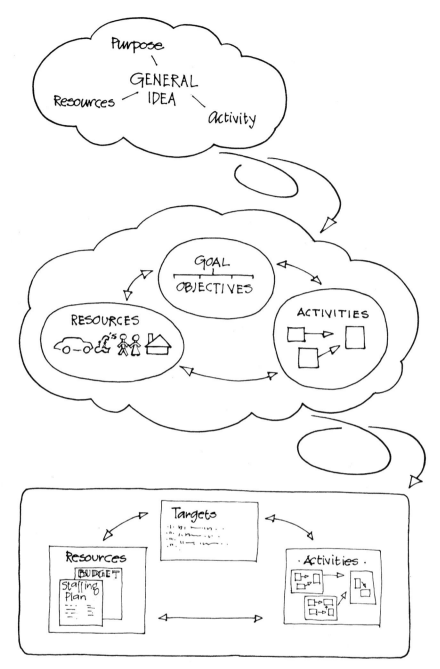

Figure 1.2   *Planning as a process of progressively clarifying and detailing what needs to be done*

QUESTION 1.1

Why is it important for there to be consistency between different objectives and between mission goals and objectives (that is, both across Figure 1.1 and up and down it)? How would such inconsistencies reveal themselves? Can inconsistency always be avoided?

Decision-making

To make a rational choice one has to be clear about the criteria on which the choice is to be made, and obtain sufficient information to enable one to assess the range of options against those criteria. This basic idea is depicted in Figure 1.3, and it appears in many different forms in management. For example, much recommended practice in areas as diverse as recruitment and selection and information system design is essentially about approximating as closely as possible to the conditions for rational choice. Indeed, management scientists provide a battery of techniques to help in finding the optimal solution to complex problems.

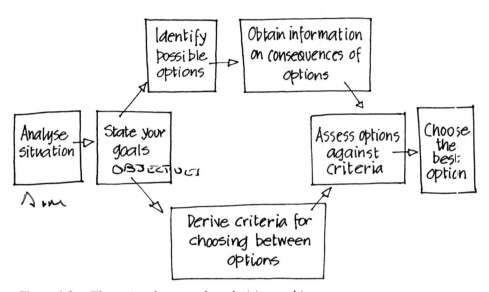

Figure 1.3   *The rational approach to decision-making*

Once again, this conception of decision-making will be immediately familiar to you. On the other hand, a moment's reflection on your own experience of taking decisions will make you realize that in practice it seldom happens in quite this way. Does this mean that you and your colleagues are muddled and disorderly, and somehow you should pull yourselves together and do one step at a time, in sequence? Not really. Often it helps to focus on particular steps in the rational model, but I doubt you will often succeed in following it through one step at a time. How our minds work and the way the normal processes of discussion, clarification and information-gathering happen mean it is unrealistic to expect decisions to emerge from a tidy series of discrete, logical steps. But we can still use the rational model to orientate, check and organize our thinking. For example, when it begins to look as though a decision is emerging, you might pause to scrutinize it and ask the following sorts of questions.

- Have we taken a broad enough view of the situation?

- Have we considered all the options?

- Do the objectives we have chosen really justify the option we prefer?

- If this *is* the option we are going for, what does that mean our objective is?

In this way, a decision can gradually be brought in line with the logic of the rational model – and presented most clearly and persuasively to others – even though *how* it actually happened was through an erratic, iterative process.

Control

The processes of control in management and organizations usually involve applications of the general idea of a *control loop* of the sort represented in Figure 1.4. This is a familiar and pervasive idea, appearing in, for example, project control, budgetary control, supervision, and so on. Control in this sense is much broader than the idea of someone being 'in charge' and having the right to issue instructions. The control loop implies that if I want to control something – be it a project, a department or just a meeting – then I need:

- a reasonably clear idea of what is intended or required

- information on performance or progress

- the capacity to be able to bring the two together if necessary, either by adjusting the plan or by taking remedial action based on a sound understanding of the situation.

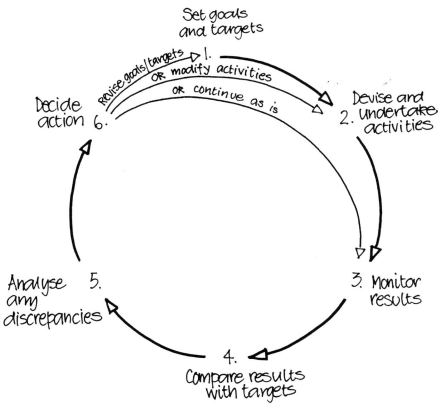

Figure 1.4   *The control loop*

Control in this sense requires an understanding of the activities involved, and it is not primarily a matter of power and authority over others. Indeed, it may not involve the control of other people at all – as, for example, when the professional partners who make up a small firm decide to spend more of their time seeking out new business because of a decline in enquiries.

QUESTION 1.2

In the light of the preceding discussion, list three ways in which a boss may not be in control of an organization, *even if* his or her subordinates do what they are told.

The idea of the control loop has surprisingly far-reaching ramifications, especially when combined with the idea of the hierarchy of objectives introduced earlier. Together, they give us the idea of there being different *levels of control*, and that organizations involve a huge variety of different, interrelated control processes, each regulating the pursuit of particular objectives. This is illustrated in Figure 1.5, which shows only two levels for one goal, so you must imagine that the same pattern is reproduced in the boxes called 'activities', or that this is just the bottom of one branch of a hierarchy that goes up and through several more layers.

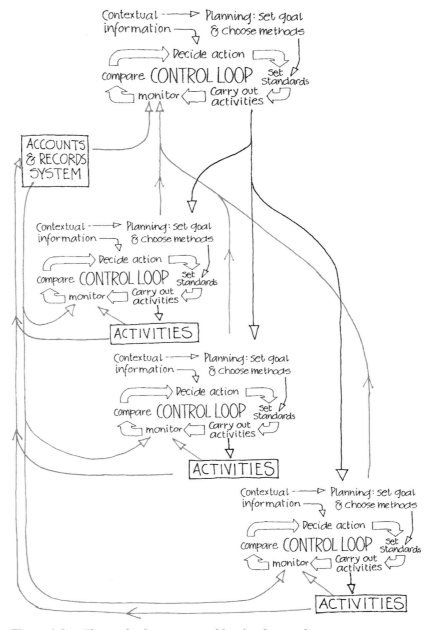

Figure 1.5 *Flows of information and levels of control*

Figure 1.5 suggests how complicated the information flows and control processes of organizations can be, and the difficulties you may experience as you are initiating activities requiring new control loops, receiving information relevant to other activities and having to decide whether and how to respond to particular discrepancies. Often the information you receive from different sources will be ambiguous, or even contradictory, or its significance will not be obvious. And there is always the problem of 'keeping lots of balls in the air at the same time'.

The same idea of different levels of control in organizations is illustrated in a much more concrete way in Table 1.1, which shows some of the monitoring, comparisons and actions involved in three different levels of a marketing organization that prepares promotional campaigns for clients.

Table 1.1   Levels of control in a marketing organization

Level	What is monitored	Standard for comparison	Action
Designer	Length and quality of draft copy (Seek colleagues' views?)	Specification provided by manager/client Own professional standards	Redraft; seek other visuals; further enquiries
	Backlog of outstanding work	Schedule for leaflets	Work late
	Number of evenings staying late	'Normal' amount of working late	Reduce future commitments; seek help; reduce quality
Publicity and Publications Manager	Status of different documents	Commitments made	Reallocate staff or contract out work
	Time and cost involved in producing leaflets, etc.	Amount originally budgeted	Revise method of estimating
	Morale and relationships	Usual pattern in team	Discuss problems
	Signs of pressure or underuse	'Fair' workloads	Reallocate staff
	Quality of work; satisfaction/ complaints of clients	Clear, attractive, persuasive, with facts and figures authenticated	Refer back to drafts or modify/redesign them oneself; discuss general issues with staff
Director	Reports of the managers involved	The results and impacts intended by the promotions/ campaigns	Discuss problems
	Interdepartmental relations	Differences handled in a professional manner; responsibilities clear	Modify responsibilities; review procedures
	Monthly budget; level of concern being expressed by Head of Finance	'Normal' uncertainty of financial situation; expected surplus in relation to target	Freeze/relax expenditure guidelines
	External developments	Current strategy	Target other client groups, instead of or as well as

T&D

ACTIVITY 1.3

Spend 10 to 15 minutes drawing up a table similar to Table 1.1 based on your own management work, that of the person or group to whom you report, and the work of a person working for you. Include just the main areas of work and do not be surprised if you find this tricky – it is often difficult to distinguish the objectives and responsibilities at different levels.

Level	What is monitored	Standard for comparison	Action
Member of your staff			
You			
Your manager			

Clearly, control at a higher level is quite different from that at a lower level – because the objectives of the two levels are different. Control at the higher level involves longer timescales, more diffuse problems and the exercise of more conceptual skills in diagnosis and planning. *In no sense is it simply a matter of 'looking over the shoulder' of people at the level below*. But neither can it ignore how the lower-level activities are proceeding. For example, if a particular campaign is rather disappointing in its results, the Director (with other staff) will have to decide whether that was because it was misconceived (under-resourced, ill-timed, poorly thought out, and so on) or because the campaign activities and documentation have been rather amateurish and uninspiring. In other words, at which level or combination of levels is the control action needed?

Thinking about the control processes in your organization in this way has important implications. First, it highlights the vital importance of communication (of all sorts) for controlling activities and resources. The more organizational levels and discrete areas of activity there are, the longer the communication channels and the more of them there have to be – with all the scope for distortion, delays and confusion that this entails. The danger is that, by the time the upper levels have worked out what is going on with the budget and issued new instructions to moderate expenditure, the situation has already deteriorated. Managers have to be wary of trying to manage by 'remote control'.

This leads to the second point: the importance of *pushing control down the organization*. The more that those involved in an activity monitor and correct their own performance, the less need there is for the group's manager to be gathering and analysing information and issuing instructions. The more self-management, the less management by someone else. The less communication in general, the quicker and more direct any communication that is needed.

However, there will be limits to this: it is not always sensible for issues that emerge in the course of particular activities to be resolved at that level, by those directly involved. The problems may involve questions of policy, or resources, or have implications for other activities that mean they have to be addressed in a broader context: no one wants precedents set or commitments entered into by one part of an organization that will undermine the work of other parts.

A third important point that comes from distinguishing different levels of control is that it can help to clarify your own and other people's roles and primary responsibilities. For example, a classic error of newly promoted supervisors or managers is devoting too much time and attention to monitoring the work of staff and making sure staff achieve their objectives – at the expense of their own objectives and responsibilities. (For example, look back to Table 1.1 and consider what would happen if the Publicity and Publications Manager spent most time monitoring and improving the quality of work, perhaps because he or she used to be a talented designer and is most comfortable doing that.) This can be particularly serious if senior managers become embroiled in lower-level issues and fail to attend to broader, longer-term developments.

Finally, by taking account of the fact that control is being exercised simultaneously in different areas and at different levels, we have *a more realistic picture of what management control actually means in practice* – and hence, too, can identify the points you need to consider if you are to control activities and resources effectively. This is shown in Figure 1.6 (overleaf), which is still derived from the basic idea of a control loop and the comparison of standards and performance, but shows that there is nothing automatic about control processes or how they work: they always depend on *attention, communication, interpretation* and *judgement*.

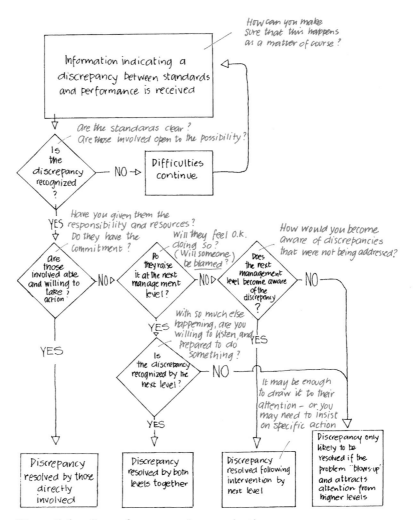

Figure 1.6   *Control processes in organizations*

ACTIVITY 1.4

Choose three tasks or areas of work for which you are or have been responsible. For each one work through Figure 1.6, examining how the activities are (or were) controlled. Make notes on any steps you could take to ensure that the control is more prompt and effective (or would be another time).

(a)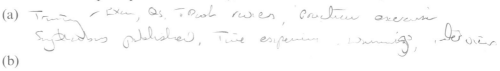

(b)

(c)

The three familiar ideas of planning, decision-making and control have taken us a long way; they are sufficient to provide the essential architecture of a wide range of organizations. It is through these managerial activities that organizations are constructed as the coherent, rational goal-seeking entities with which we are familiar. So surely they are what management is all about?

The short answer is 'No'. At best, the picture that has been presented is one-sided and simplistic; at worst, it is dangerously out of date and misleading.

1.3 Directing or empowering?

One criticism of the traditional view of management, as set out in Section 1.2, focuses on the way in which organizations and management have changed. The argument is that it is no longer helpful to think of managers primarily in terms of *deciding and controlling things within hierarchies* – although, of course, lots of that still goes on. Management is now more often and more fundamentally about *enabling* effective action, *influencing* and *team-working* within organizational and interorganizational *networks*. This is sometimes called the *empowering* view of management, and it was clearly articulated by Rosabeth Moss Kanter in a famous article summarized in Box 1.2.

Box 1.2   The new managerial work

Managerial work is undergoing such enormous and rapid change that many managers are reinventing their profession as they go. With little precedent to guide them, they are watching hierarchy fade away and the clear distinctions of title, task, department, even corporation, blur. Faced with extraordinary levels of complexity and interdependency, they watch traditional sources of power erode and the old motivational tools lose their magic.

The cause is obvious. Competitive pressures are forcing corporations to adopt new flexible strategies and structures. Many of these are familiar: acquisitions and divestitures aimed at more focused combinations of business activities, reductions in management staff and levels of hierarchy, increased use of performance-based rewards. Other strategies are less common but have an even more profound effect. In a growing number of companies, for example, horizontal ties between peers are replacing vertical ties as channels of activity and communication. Companies are asking corporate staffs and functional departments to play a more strategic role with greater cross-departmental collaboration. Some organizations are turning themselves nearly inside out – buying formerly internal services from outside suppliers, forming strategic alliances and supplier–customer partnerships that bring external relationships inside where they can influence company policy and practice. I call these emerging practices 'post entrepreneurial' because they involve the application of entrepreneurial creativity and flexibility to established businesses.

Such changes come highly recommended by the experts who urge organizations to become leaner, less bureaucratic, more entrepreneurial. But so far, theorists have given scant attention to the dramatically altered realities of managerial work in these transformed corporations. We don't even have good words to describe the new relationships. 'Superiors' and 'subordinates' hardly seem accurate, and even 'bosses' and 'their people' imply more control and ownership than managers today actually possess. On top of it all, career paths are no longer straightforward and predictable but have become idiosyncratic and confusing.

Some managers experience the new managerial work as a loss of power because much of their authority used to come from hierarchical position. Now that everything seems negotiable by everyone, they are confused about how to mobilise and motivate staff. For other managers, the shift in roles and tasks offers greater personal power.

(Source: Kanter, 1989)

The empowering approach is a bigger change for some organizations than others. Position, title and authority were never very important in many not-for-profit organizations

Since this article was published many other people have come to the same conclusions. The sources, nature and extent of the changes in managerial roles are worth considering closely, so you should now read the article 'Managing 21st century network organizations' by Snow *et al.* in the *Managing Change* course reader.

QUESTION 1.3

What is the key difference between Snow *et al.*'s views of organizations and management and the views set out in Section 1.2? In what respects are they similar?

ACTIVITY 1.5

Consider the extent to which Snow *et al.'s* observations apply to your own organization and work.

(a) Which of the drivers for change are also affecting your organization? What other forces are relevant (especially if you work in a public or not-for-profit agency)?

(b) What sort of network organization do you see as emerging in or around your organization?

(c) Do you play the role of a broker – and, if you do, what sort of broker? Which of the entries in your Activity Log could be described as brokering activities?

These ideas raise some awkward questions about the traditional view of organizations as rational, coherent entities. It is doubtful, for example, whether the organizations described by Snow *et al.* arose as the result of deliberate organizational design. The networks on which they are based were not so much the implementation of a chief executive's grand plan as the result of several different responses to a variety of intense pressures – and everyone involved was still struggling to understand these new ways of organizing. Likewise, it is doubtful whether the decisions made by the broker–managers in these organizations would bear much relationship to the rational model described in Section 1.2. The complexity of the issues they face and the pace of change mean they cannot gather the information needed to evaluate even a few options at all rigorously – and, even if they could, it is doubtful whether they and/or their organizations and/or collaborators would have shared, consistent and stable enough objectives to provide the clear selection criteria required by the rational model of decision-making.

This is not to claim that the managers involved were behaving irrationally. Later in the course we shall examine these issues in more depth and argue that managers frequently ignore the rational model of decision-making *and often they are right to do so*. The point is that the nature and extent of rationality in organizations and management is far from straightforward.

The views you have just been considering are now advocated by many management writers and consultants. But this does not mean they are right. In fact, they remain decidedly controversial – as you can discover by looking at the scathing attack on these views in the article 'Managerial leadership: the key to good organization' by Elliott Jaques in the *Managing Learning* course reader. Read it now, and answer the following questions to check that you have understood the key points.

QUESTION 1.4

(a) Why, according to Jaques, is managerial hierarchy essential in modern organizations? *Because it is intrinsic of the accountability. Right no of layers, right degree of accountability*

(b) Give three reasons why Jaques thinks the notion of hierarchy has gone out of favour. *Japan, Improvement, IT*

(c) What does Jaques see as the weakness in the concepts of empowerment and networking? *Accountability*

(d) How would Jaques respond to the criticism that he is endorsing essentially undemocratic forms of organization and management? *People accept it - need it*

(e) What does Jaques propose as the key steps to effective organization and management? *Leadership relationship, personnel structure*

This debate is examined in more detail in Section 1 of the video-cassette where Elliott Jacques and other leading theorists and practitioners set out their views.

The argument between traditional and empowering views of management will crop up again at various points in the course, because it is a far-reaching and complex debate. It is not simply a theoretical matter that the practical manager can safely leave to the researchers. In fact, the argument is being played out on a daily basis in organizations across the world. In all kinds of ways, these ideas are shaping the thinking of consultants and managers, and are thus becoming embodied in training programmes and organizational arrangements.

1.4 Rational or fashionable?

Another critique of the traditional, directive view of management challenges its claim to rationality. According to this argument, the traditional view slides imperceptibly from the assertion that managers *try* to make their organizations as efficient and effective as possible to the proposition that the practices they embody in organizations are *actually* efficient and effective. In other words, it presents a positive and appealing view of managers, quietly screening out the possibility that *they might be mistaken about what works well in organizations*.

Since managers are fallible human beings, this suggestion is only interesting if it can also be shown that their mistakes are, not infrequently, significant and systematic (rather than minor and random) – or that managers persist in using methods that have been shown to be ineffective. This may be thought rather unlikely: if the organization concerned operated in a competitive market, or if its performance was otherwise open to comparative scrutiny, such mistakes would quickly become obvious. But this only shows that *the widely shared misconceptions will be more likely to survive*.

Are there such misconceptions? Arguably, yes. Indeed, *the range of possible examples is quite extensive*. Would you believe, for example, that in the UK over the course of 25 years many attempts, often highly sophisticated, have repeatedly failed to verify the efficiency gains that are supposed to result from mergers and acquisitions? This has caused many researchers to conclude that these gains are simply not realized and that the economic justification for mergers and acquisitions is frequently unsound.

That said, I readily acknowledge that such claims are controversial. Indeed, they are *bound* to be controversial – for important reasons which are best explained by considering a case in point. I shall use performance-related pay (PRP) for this purpose.

Between one-half and two-thirds of UK companies and the vast majority of US firms use some form of PRP for at least some of their workers. It is less common in continental Europe and Japan.

PRP is intended to encourage good individual performance by rewarding it with extra pay. In other words, the amount a person is paid does not depend just on their position in the organization but on the quantity and quality of the results they achieve in that position. PRP provides a good example of the questionable rationality of organizational practices. Those who make the decisions about pay schemes, presumably among the more capable and hard-headed controllers of organizations, would be expected to use the most effective methods available. PRP is widely used, yet there is little evidence that it is effective. ·

Performance-related pay is introduced for one main reason: to get people to work harder. This simple idea may be expressed in all sorts of ways: 'to align the individual's efforts with those of the organization'; 'to change the culture by rewarding appropriate behaviour'; 'to secure a more delegated and performance-related culture'; and so on. Despite this variety, the overall goals are to motivate the people in the organization to function more efficiently. By this means the organization may meet its goals of reducing costs and increasing profitability and competitiveness. To what extent are these goals achieved? Here are some quotations from studies of PRP.

> ... the research has consistently shown that any contingent payment system tends to undermine intrinsic motivation.
>
> (Deci and Ryan, 1985)

> ... the benefits most often claimed for PRP are not met in practice.
>
> (Institute of Manpower Studies, 1993)

> As for productivity, at least two dozen studies over the last three decades have conclusively shown that people who expect to receive a reward for completing a task or for doing that task successfully simply do not perform as well as those who expect no reward at all.
>
> (Kohn, 1993)

> There are a number of difficulties surrounding PRP. First, there is very little evidence which confirms the positive effects desired; indeed, there is research which points clearly to possible negative consequences. Second, there is evidence which illustrates the considerable operational difficulties involved in implementing and operating PRP. Third, there is a failure to meet principles which stem from relevant psychological theory.
>
> (Williams, 1998)

> If one ignores for a moment the substantial body of evidence which casts doubts on the link between pay and performance, the case for performance related pay sounds very plausible.
>
> (Sisson and Storey, 2000)

The nub of the problem is this. There is significant evidence that the effect of PRP on motivation and performance is, at best, neutral and, at worst, adverse – and yet PRP continues to be seen as an important means of motivating better performance.

"Boss. how are you measuring my performance when more and more of us are doing cross-functional work!"

Box 1.3 is based on a controversial article by Alfie Kohn published in the *Harvard Business Review* in 1993.

Box 1.3   Why performance-related pay does not work

When researchers ask people what motivates them to perform well in their organization they typically get responses that place enjoyment of the job, a sense of achievement, and recognition at the top of the list. Money appears only in sixth or seventh place. This seems to be true at all levels within organizations and has been shown repeatedly over several decades. The evidence also shows that there is no typical pattern of motivation: people vary enormously, both from each other and at different times in their lives. There are a number of motivators that have been identified by psychologists. *Intrinsic motivators* come from within a person, and include things like the feeling of doing something worth while, the sense of achievement and the excitement of a challenge. Other rewards and motivations come from outside: money, status, praise and recognition. These are *extrinsic motivators*. Performance-related pay is clearly an extrinsic motivator. But why does it not produce the results claimed for it?

Behaviourist theory, based on laboratory work with animals, has shown that animals will modify their behaviour to gain rewards. The theory behind PRP schemes is that human beings respond in the same way. The theory is attractively simple: reward people for performing well and they will continue to perform well; those who are not performing well will learn to perform well if offered an incentive. The trouble with this theory is that human motivation is more complicated than is suggested by simple analogies with animal experiments. When it comes to lasting change in attitudes and behaviour, extrinsic motivators are strikingly ineffective. They succeed in producing *temporary compliance*, but not long-term changes in motivation and commitment. Against this background, there are good reasons for believing that PRP will *never* work except in the short term. Intrinsic motivation, by contrast, is much more effective for achieving long-term commitment and high performance. There are six reasons why PRP schemes are bound to fail.

Pay is not a motivator. Too little pay is demotivating, and if people are poorly paid they will not be motivated to perform well or identify with the organization. They see poor pay as a sign that they are not valued by the organization, which is what really matters to them. But there is no evidence to suggest that increasing someone's pay will bring a corresponding improvement in motivation and performance.

Rewards are a covert form of punishment. Most managers recognize that fear and coercion are demotivating, producing a poor working environment and poor performance. The trouble with PRP is that *not* receiving a reward is often indistinguishable from being punished, and can produce bitter resentment if the reward has been worked for or is expected. The effect on morale is exactly the same as that of fear and coercion.

Rewards disrupt team-work. 'Everyone is pressuring the system for individual gain. No one is improving the system for collective gain. Eventually, the system will crash.' Organizational life depends so much on co-operation and team-work that the competition for reward can be disastrous, as each person tries to outdo their colleagues. The award of bonus payments produces jealousy and resentment which are a very effective way of destroying working relationships. Employees may be tempted to conceal problems and to present themselves as competent to their supervisors.

Other things affect performance. It may well be that other issues prevent employees from performing well. These issues may include a lack of resources, poor facilities or overload. Relying on PRP simply obscures these difficulties. It impedes the ability of managers to manage and will not have the desired effect.

PRP may encourage *excessive* risk-taking. It has been argued that the large bonuses and share options available to some chief executives encourage them to take excessive risks. If a gamble pays off, they will earn huge amounts: if it starts to go wrong, they will leave for another job before the extent of the damage is obvious. This has been suggested as a factor in several major business failures. Of course, the chief executives may not have been influenced in this way – but if PRP works, perhaps they should have been!

PRP discourages risk-taking. As soon as you set criteria for performance, people will work towards maximizing on those criteria. They will be much less inclined to explore new ways of doing things. Instead, people work towards the goals that will yield the rewards. It motivates people to get rewards, not to improve the performance of the organization as a whole.

Rewards undermine interest. Extrinsic rewards undermine intrinsic motivation. This is especially true of complex and interesting tasks. One theory is that people feel more controlled when offered extrinsic rewards for good performance and that this reduces their intrinsic motivation. Other theories claim that it sends a message to employees that they read as, 'If they have to bribe me then it must be something I wouldn't want to do.' Psychologists have shown that the larger the incentive, the more negative the perception of the task (Freedman *et al.*, 1992).

Performance-related pay does not work in the way it is supposed to. As Kohn says, 'It is difficult to overstate the extent to which most managers and the people who advise them believe in the redemptive power of rewards.' There seems to be a powerful underlying belief that extrinsic 'carrots' work. A belief that 'for pay to mean anything, it must be linked to performance. Without that belief, pay becomes nothing more than entitlement, a job nothing more than a sinecure' (Stewart, 1993).

(Source: adapted from Kohn, 1993)

Kohn's article is one of many pieces of work that carry the same message. But if PRP is ineffective and damaging, why do rational managers not recognize this fact? The obvious answer – represented in Figure 1.7 – is that the immediate results of introducing PRP confirm the 'common-sense' beliefs on which PRP rests.

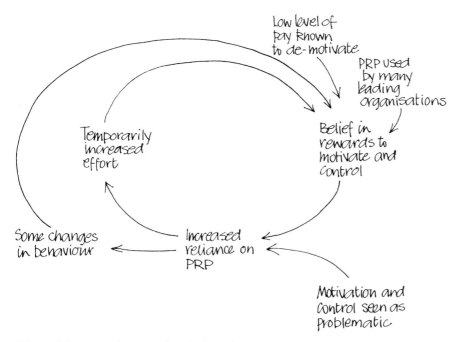

Figure 1.7   *Justifications for the belief in performance-related pay*

However, there must be more to it than this. After all, if increased effort is only temporary, this would surely be noticed and the belief in PRP questioned. Or would it? In fact, our beliefs are not so easily overturned. Rather, they have a strong tendency to be *self-sealing*. They shape our perceptions so that we interpret events in ways that fit with the beliefs (and we simply overlook or forget facts that are obtrusively inconvenient). So we can suppose that those committed to PRP will attribute their staff's appropriate behaviour to the beneficial effects of PRP – even if it would have occurred anyway. Moreover, inappropriate behaviour can be attributed to an *insufficiency* of PRP – perhaps the procedures are not adequate, or perhaps a greater proportion of salary needs to be awarded in this way. Indeed, if the motivation, control and performance of staff remain problematic, this may well be seen as a reason for giving more emphasis to PRP. 'It worked before, so let's try it again.' This situation is represented in Figure 1.8.

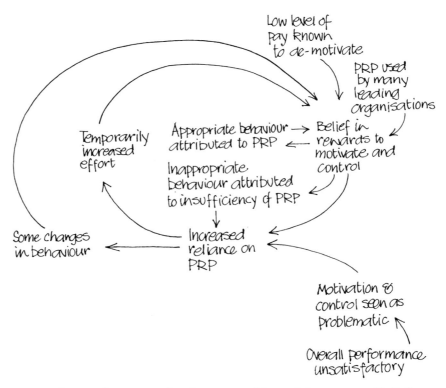

Figure 1.8   *Performance-related pay as a self-sustaining system of beliefs*

B800 student contributions to electronic debate on the topic suggest that these negative effects of individual PRP continue to be experienced.

Meanwhile, if Kohn's analysis is to be believed, the actual longer-term effects of PRP are likely to be building up – with reduced team-work, risk-taking, intrinsic motivation and morale all off-setting such (temporary) gains as may have followed a greater reliance on PRP. The overall picture is represented in Figure 1.9.

So the 'performance' of PRP turns out to be a complicated issue. Indeed, it is probably more complicated than Kohn allows: his analysis of motivation is rather simplistic, and PRP itself can take many forms.

There is also evidence that PRP may have very little impact of any kind because it is frequently implemented so half-heartedly! The relationship between pay and motivation is examined more closely in Book 2.

Nevertheless, this brief survey of research findings is sufficient to raise questions about the substantive rationality of the use of PRP in many contexts. It would certainly be hard to argue that the increase in the use of PRP in the UK in recent years is a result of its proven success. Indeed, what many practical managers see as 'common sense' and 'good practice' looks suspiciously like an ideological fashion.

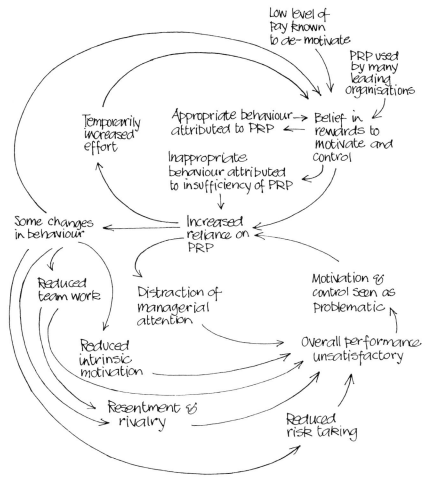

Figure 1.9   *Performance-related pay: the longer-term consequences*

However, the main point here is a much more general one, and PRP is simply an example: namely, that it is often extremely difficult to tell whether a particular management practice or approach works. This is because:

- A huge number of factors affect the performance of an organization or a department; the impact of a new approach or technique may be lost in the effects of other internal and external changes.

- Organizations and the work they do vary enormously – an approach that works in some circumstances may be unhelpful or damaging in others.

- Most management approaches and practices involve a general idea that can be applied in very different ways, some of which may be effective while others are not. (PRP systems, for example, may assess performance more or less carefully, and involve a larger or a smaller proportion of total pay.)

- Impressions concerning the success or failure of particular approaches often reflect the prior assumptions and expectations of those involved. A serious assessment of advantages and disadvantages has to take account of the tendency for beliefs to be *self-sealing*, especially when managers are committed to a particular view.

So, judging whether a particular approach is really effective in particular circumstances will often be very difficult. Moreover, ineffective practices can still *appear* natural and sensible, especially if they are consistent with other widely-held beliefs. In short, the rationality of organizational arrangements is frequently problematic.

Part of the problem is the degree of complexity found in organizations. As the course progresses you will encounter such complexity frequently, and be introduced to a range of concepts, and techniques such as diagramming, to help you explore and deal with it.

ACTIVITY 1.6

What effects do you think PRP would have, or does have, on (a) your staff and (b) yourself? What makes you think so?

1.5 Conclusions

This session started with the traditional, functional view of management, and asserted that it is still a powerful force, shaping organizations and encompassing many aspects of managerial activity. Two different criticisms of that view have also been presented, each in its own way presenting an important challenge. These criticisms highlight what will be two recurring themes in this book and the course as a whole.

First, many of the plausible and familiar generalizations that are made about management and about how to manage turn out to be controversial or problematic, especially in a rapidly changing world. This does not mean we cannot generalize about management – we can and must, for it is through generalizations (theories) that we understand and learn. The point is that the generalizations have to be appraised and must not be accepted uncritically, not least because there are often opposing theories and views on offer.

Second, whether and to what extent conflicting theories and prescriptions are relevant and enlightening for you depends very heavily on circumstances. Only you are in a position to interpret the circumstances of your work and make these judgements.

Objectives

After studying this session you should be able to:

- Explain, in your own words and using examples from your own experience, the ways in which your organization tries to embody rational methods of planning, decision-making and control in its structure and operation.

- Critically appraise the relevance of the 'directive' and 'empowering' views of management in relation to your own organization and your own role.

- Explain, using performance-related pay or other appropriate examples, why beliefs in the effectiveness of management practices may be only loosely related to their actual effects.

Contents

2.1 Introduction

Session 1 considered management in abstract and impersonal terms; it was about management 'out there', management as it is supposed to be. This session is very different: it is about managers as people and the experience of managing; it is about management as it really happens and how you cope with the day-to-day pressures of your work in the context of your life and career. It is, ultimately, about *managing yourself* – and whether we need to consider putting our own house in order, even as we manage others.

The aims of this session are to:

* Highlight some of the common traps, dilemmas and pitfalls of managerial work.

* Clarify some of the personal choices we all face as managers.

* Consider the contribution to personal effectiveness provided by the ideas of time management.

2.2 Managerial work and the superficiality trap

In 1980, reporting on work done earlier, Henry Mintzberg said that managers work hard and long. It is a safe bet that since then the amount and the pace of managers' work have increased. It may therefore seem unnecessary to ask why managers work so hard and so long. But this is a revealing question: the answer points to some important features of the manager's role. The manager's job is inherently open-ended: 'there are really no tangible mileposts where he [*sic*] can stop and say, "now my job is finished" ... the manager is a person with a perpetual preoccupation' (Mintzberg, 1980). Since the work is never finished, the manager can never finish.

But what about the type of activity that goes on during these long periods of work? Mintzberg found that, when he analysed what managers actually did, no activity patterns were evident, except one: the work occurred in very short episodes, was highly fragmented, frequently interrupted and brief in duration. Why? Mintzberg argues that managers themselves determined the duration of their activities. He accounts for this by a process of conditioning, whereby the managers:

'The manager is a person with a perpetual preoccupation' (Mintzberg, 1980)

> ... are encouraged by the realities of [their] work to develop a particular personality – to overload [themselves] with work, to do things abruptly, to avoid wasting time, to participate only when the value of participation is tangible, to avoid too great an involvement with one issue. To be superficial is, no doubt, an occupational hazard of managerial work. In order to succeed, the manager must, presumably, become proficient at his [*sic*] superficiality.
>
> (Mintzberg, 1980)

This quotation is important because it raises for the first time a point to which we shall return later, that is, that managers may be encouraged by circumstances, and by their own preferences, to behave skilfully in ways that are also in an important sense *incompetent*. Such skill can be counter-productive – as Mintzberg puts it, managers may become proficient at their superficiality.

Mintzberg (1980) makes some other interesting observations on the realities of managerial work.

- He notes it is commonly held that managers are systematic, reflective planners, but asserts that the evidence shows that managers like, and gravitate towards, the active aspects of their work – 'activities that are current, specific, and well-defined and that are non-routine'. The managers' environment, and their own preferences, do not encourage planning, reflection and analysis but instead encourage 'adaptive information manipulators who prefer the live, concrete situation ... [and] live action'.

- He finds that managers prefer verbal media and informal means of communication and, not surprisingly, spend substantial time with subordinates, far less with superiors. 'Subordinates made a variety of requests of the managers, largely for authorization, information, in the form of operating reports, "instant communication", briefings on problems and opportunities, ideas, trade gossip and so on.'

- He analyses the extent to which managers control their own work or respond to the requests of others – the extent to which they are *reactive* or *proactive*. He points out that the reality differs from the popular conception in that most managers are unable to control or choose most of their activities. Nevertheless, he believes that the ability to achieve some control over one's work is one mark of a successful manager.

Mintzberg's analysis is important in two main ways. First, it shows that it is not enough to describe what managers *ought* to do on the basis of general descriptions of their undoubtedly vital functions. It is important to understand the pressures they experience and the traps in which they risk being ensnared.

> The manager [is] overburdened with work. With the increasing complexity of modern organizations and their problems he [*sic*] is destined to become more so. He is driven to brevity, fragmentation and superficiality in his tasks, yet he cannot easily debate them because of the nature of his information. And he can do little to increase his available time or significantly enhance his power to manage. Furthermore, he is driven to focus on that which is current and tangible in his work even though the complex problems facing many organizations call for reflection and a far-sighted perspective.
>
> (Mintzberg, 1980)

Mintzberg regards these characteristics as negative and unhelpful, and ill-suited to the demands of contemporary managerial work. I agree with that assessment.

Second, Mintzberg describes what he calls a 'loop' in which managers are caught – a vicious circle in which managers respond to constant environmental demands reactively by working in fragmented, superficial ways. These responses are managers' ways of 'solving' their work pressures; but they make matters worse because they are unsuccessful solutions. Yet this does not stop managers from using them – on the contrary, when they do not work they continue to use them. Clearly, managers are good at and committed to these ways of working – they become 'proficient at superficiality'. Here then is a paradox: a solution that does not work, yet is repeated endlessly and causes the manager difficulties and stresses (too much work, time problems, and so on). Managers cope skilfully with the unrelenting pressure – but in ways which, far from improving their lot, actually reproduce the very difficulties they curse.

ACTIVITY 2.1

(a) To what extent does your experience of managers and managing match Mintzberg's analysis? How comfortable do you feel with the following characteristics?

A lot	Somewhat	Not much		I generally enjoy this	I do not like this
☑	☐	☐	Fast pace of work	☑	☐
☑	☐	☐	Many interruptions	☐	☑
☐	☑	☐	Brevity, variety and fragmentation of activities	☐	☑
☑	☐	☐	Lots of verbal (rather than written) contacts	☑	☐
☐	☑	☐	Lots of time in scheduled meetings	☐	☑

(b) In what ways does your Activity Log confirm Mintzberg's account – and in what ways does it differ from it?

Agendas
for inspection

(c) Can you recall occasions when managers wasted their own time as a result of doing things 'on the hoof'? (For example, they made decisions on an inadequate basis and had to reconsider them later; they failed to anticipate predictable problems and then had to spend much more time recovering the situation; they had to do work again, or had to change direction and write off work that had already been done; or they wasted time in meetings for which those present were inadequately prepared; and so on.)

(d) Are you aware of putting off the quieter and more individual think-work of planning, analysing, and reading and writing reports?

Yes

(e) How far are you and your colleagues able to be proactive in your work, choosing the issues you will address? Or is nearly all your time spent reacting to events and responding to demands from others?

No

(f) If the manager's job is never done, how do *you* decide when to stop?

Plans, Programmes, Resources, contingency

It may be that your own work experience is not as apparently pressured and fragmented as the managers Mintzberg studied. Nevertheless, it would be surprising if what you do from hour to hour and day to day is routinely ordered and systematic. The question of how you make the best of this sort of work and avoid the worst excesses of the superficiality trap is considered in Section 2.4.

Mintzberg's account raises more questions about the rationality of the management activity discussed in Session 1. How does the rational model of decision-making, with its systematic and considered evaluation of the alternatives, fit in with the untidy realities of managerial behaviour? The answer can only be 'with great difficulty.' It could even be argued that, in the great majority of their day-to-day decisions, managers do not even approximate to the rational model.

So how do managers decide? Are they being irrational? An important alternative perspective on managerial decision-making is provided by the notion of limited or 'bounded' rationality. This notion starts by recognizing that managers have neither the time nor the intellectual capacity – and this is not a criticism – to foresee and weigh up the full consequences of all the options. So, in many situations, they aim for acceptable or satisfactory decisions, rather than the best or optimal decision aspired to by the rational model of decision-making. They do not seek good solutions to all the issues they face, simply solutions that are *good enough*. The essential dynamics of such decision-making are represented in Figure 2.1 (and contrast sharply with those of the rational model you met in Figure 1.3).

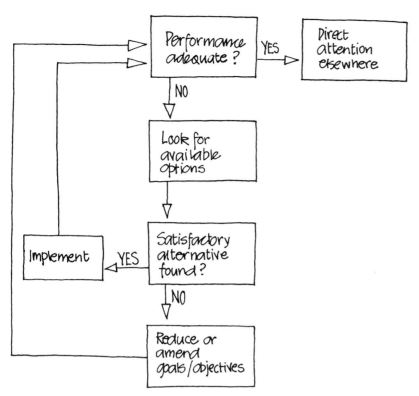

Figure 2.1   *'Bounded rationality' decision-making*

Managers behaving in this way try out the solutions that come readily to hand – and, if none of these is satisfactory, they reduce their aspirations and settle for less. In this way, they try to make the best use of their limited time and attention, progressing as many issues as they can. To be sure, such behaviour carries the risks that Mintzberg highlights, but it is certainly not irrational. It may represent a more modest conception of rationality, but it is realistic and possesses a certain logic all the same.

Whereas Figure 1.3 presents a normative model – how things should be done – Figure 2.1 is a descriptive model, one that tries to encapsulate what actually happens. Both sorts of model play their part in management, but it is important not to mix them up: Figure 1.3 is not a description and Figure 2.1 is not a recommendation.

QUESTION 2.1

(a) Why is it sometimes right not to seek the best decision?

Improvement rate, flexibility of options, what is best?

(b) In what circumstances would it be right to make 'boundedly rational' decisions? In what circumstances would it be appropriate to try to be fully rational? What factors are relevant to the choice?

2.3 Successful or effective?

The rational view of organizations assumes that effective managers are successful and that successful managers are effective. But what if this were not the case? What if you could choose between being a *good* manager and *getting ahead* as a manager? This may seem fanciful – but if your work is unstructured and involves considerable discretion, you have to decide the amount of time and energy that you put into its different aspects. If some activities produce better results, while others lead to faster promotion, you may already have been choosing, knowingly or unknowingly, what sort of manager you will be.

You should now read the article by Fred Luthans, 'Successful versus effective real managers', in Supplementary Resources: People 1.

QUESTION 2.2

What features of this research mean its conclusions cannot be dismissed lightly? Nevertheless, what grounds are there for doubting whether its conclusions apply nowadays, or to you and your situation?

ACTIVITY 2.2

Consider how Luthans' conclusions relate to your own observations and thinking.

(a) Can you distinguish between successful managers, effective managers and those who are both successful and effective? Are you aware of any differences in the way they allocate their time and attention – and do those differences fit in with Luthans' conclusions?

(b) How would your colleagues view you? Is this confirmed by an analysis of your Activity Log?

(c) Are you ever aware of choosing between networking activities (to make sure you are noticed) and people management and communication activities (to help the work and morale)? Will an awareness of the behavioural differences between successful and effective managers mean you think differently about any such choices in the future?

Luthans' study reminds us of the obvious: that managers are human, that they have values and interests of their own. These values and interests do not simply appear in a predilection for networking, nor do they concern only one's long-term career. In fact, our interests are shaped to a considerable extent by the organizational context in which we work and the professional and other identities we have built up. As managers in particular positions with particular experience, we have our own distinct perspectives and concerns; our own view of what is needed for the organization to prosper; our own responsibilities and network of relationships; and our own aspirations for how changed organizational arrangements might offer advantages to our projects, our staff or ourselves. We seek to promote these views, to encourage others to see things either as we do or in ways that are consonant with our concerns.

This means we need to know what is going on around us: we check out what other people are thinking, and 'compare notes' with others we trust about what was 'really' going on in the meeting, or about who is in favour with whom. We promote the activities and initiatives we think important by entering tacit alliances, by discreet lobbying of the powerful, and by framing our concerns in terms that will command the widest support – perhaps in relation to widely accepted organizational problems, or legitimate organizational values, such as growth and quality. We do not lie and deceive, of course, but we may be less than frank as we edit and 'gloss' what we say in the light of years of experience.

This is everyday organizational politics. Far from being frowned upon as the scheming of Machiavellian manipulators, it is *expected* of us. Managers have to be able to fight their corners – while still maintaining, as far as possible, a good working relationship with those who see things differently.

> Because individuals with distinct perspectives and political concerns rarely reach complete agreement about ends and means, compromise outcomes are often negotiated or bargains struck about favours to be exchanged at different times. Alliances will be formed, some relatively stable and enduring, others relatively short-term. The energetic will spend considerable effort and time in finding out what others want and think on a particular issue ... They will 'chat up' those they regard as powerful, not for any particular purpose but still with some strategic conception that such activities will bear fruit later in some particular context. And they will do these things because they seek, as reasonable men and women, to pursue what they regard as right and best.
>
> (Eden *et al.*, 1983)

So, management is also about interests, both personal and sectional, and the political dimension of managerial work is pervasive and important. It is not some distasteful aberration from pure rationality – as a purely functional view might imply. But, like so many other aspects of management, the politics can be more or less enjoyable for the participants, and can be conducted more or less skilfully. This topic is discussed in greater detail in the Organizations Block.

ACTIVITY 2.3

How conscious are you of the political 'under-life' of management, and what is your attitude towards it? For example:

(a) Do you feel impatient about having to engage in politics, or do you enjoy it and perhaps take some pride in your political skills? As far as you can recall, how many of the entries in your Activity Log involved a distinct political dimension?

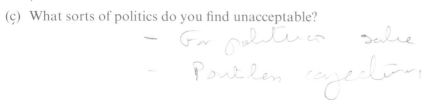

(b) Are you critical of political manoeuvring by others? Do you wish they were more adept (for example, less brutal or more open)? Or does the whole idea dismay you?

(c) What sorts of politics do you find unacceptable?

For many people 'to politick' is an irregular verb:

> *I try to help others recognize where their interests really lie;*
>
> *you try to persuade and strike deals;*
>
> *he or she tries to scheme and manipulate.*

The inevitable tensions that surround organizational decision-making can be handled more or less constructively. This is one of the most important and most difficult aspects of managerial work, and it can make a huge difference to relationships, atmosphere and morale.

2.4 Coping with the pressure

You will get more out of this section if you have already tried to use some time management ideas, from *The MBA Handbook* or from a training course.

Managers experience pressure and stress in their work for many reasons – including apparent threats to their interests or careers. The unrelenting workload noted by Mintzberg is often felt to be a major stress factor, and it has given rise to an extensive popular literature offering a body of ideas and practices known as *time management*, which aims to help managers cope with their workload. How useful is this literature? Can it help managers to avoid the traps of superficiality and stress, to be more effective, and to maintain a balanced life? Alternatively, is it a dubious mix of exhortation, slogans and anecdotes that promises far more than it can deliver – and can even make matters *worse* by encouraging people to blame themselves for not coping with unreasonable workloads? Perhaps the question is: 'If time management is such a good idea, why do we find it so difficult to apply?'.

The essentials of time management

The general philosophy of time management can be summed up in the phrase 'work smarter, not harder'. The idea is that, by examining our working practices and following several common-sense guidelines in a disciplined fashion, we can all achieve significantly more than is possible through the rather haphazard work patterns that tend to emerge if we simply respond to the demands and pressures of our work.

This syndrome echoes some of Mintzberg's observations about managerial work, but in a chaotic and ill-disciplined way. The 'fire-fighting' manager can hardly be called skilful in his or her superficiality.

It is useful to distinguish three different ways in which managers may misuse their time. The first is known as the *fire-fighting* syndrome (or, less kindly, as the 'headless chicken' style of management). This approach is characterized by personal disorganization and inefficient work practices: the 'fire-fighting' manager is surprised by deadlines, cannot find documents, does work that could be done better by other people, causes difficulties for others by neglecting routine paperwork and communication, does not explain properly what is needed when he or she does delegate, is unprepared for meetings, and generally lurches from one self-inflicted crisis to another.

In more severe cases, and over prolonged periods, this leads to a general inability to concentrate and make decisions, and it is often associated with ill health, excessive alcohol consumption, and relationship problems in and out of work.

The second way of using time ineffectively is to become *stressed* at work. The more tired and run-down I am, the worse my judgement: all sorts of decisions and activities appear terribly important; I feel I have to get involved and do more; I become hopelessly overoptimistic about what I shall be able to get through ... and so the tendency is to become even more overloaded, to work less effectively but for even longer hours, and to become more stressed. By contrast, after a holiday even major problems do not 'get to us' in the same way – we simply get on with doing the best we can.

Stress can therefore be both the result and the cause of poor time management: ineffective attempts to cope with a heavy workload often result in stress which further reduces the manager's ability to cope.

The third way of misusing time is much less obvious than the other two: it simply involves *confusing what is urgent with what is important*. This is the well-organized manager's way of using time ineffectively and it is quite compatible with a tidy desk and the appearance of proficiency. All that is necessary is a responsive orientation and a short-term outlook. The manager then responds and reacts, but the things that really matter get squeezed out, neglected or simply overlooked.

So what does time management recommend? First, managers have to be organized and self-disciplined in terms of recording commitments, keeping in touch with their assistants, dealing with the paperwork regularly, and so on.

This may well involve spending time to save time by creating systems or procedures to handle particular matters. The problem is that when we are falling behind it is tempting to try to catch up by cutting back on the time spent on staying organized. This means that we start to work less effectively, so the problem gets worse.

Second, managers can make good use of their time only if they are clear about what they are trying to achieve. Without this you have no basis for deciding the relative importance of the many different calls on your time. Deciding on priorities is particularly important if you are in a situation where you cannot do everything that you would like to do, or that some people expect you to do. In these cases, it is essential to *face up to this* and to *decide* what is not going to be done – instead of just leaving it to happen by chance. This involves standing back and analysing the different sorts of tasks in which you are engaged. Managers need to go *behind* the long lists of 'things that must be done' to clarify the important underlying objectives and identify a limited number of *key work areas*. Each of these work areas will be important in its own right, so you cannot, for any length of time, neglect one in favour of the others. But within these work areas you should be able to determine the relative priority of different activities.

Third, managers need to *structure* their time. This means breaking up your time into blocks which are then allocated to different sorts of activities. In this way you can use the times of the day or the week when you have most energy for the tasks requiring most effort or concentration; you can match the type of work you do to the prevailing conditions and limit the time you spend on different activities. And, since the aim is not just to get as much important work done as you can but also to keep yourself in good shape, you need to schedule regular exercise and relaxation into your weekly routine and make sure you take holidays.

Fourth, managers need to negotiate their commitments. Scaling down the demands coming from a particular source may be difficult and take time, particularly if prior commitments have to be phased out or if work has to be reorganized. But it may be that those making new demands simply do not have a realistic understanding of what your work involves. Negotiating commitments – and saying 'No' if necessary – is the best way to ensure that people understand your work and encourage realism about what you can and cannot undertake.

Fifth, regular work planning is strongly recommended. Hence, the use of personal organizers, year planners, bar charts, project planning software and other planning tools. This does not mean that the advocates of time

There is evidence that the number of hours worked by British managers rose in the 1990s – and that they are working significantly longer than their counterparts in the rest of Europe.

I have always had a structured approach, with my secretary as a gatekeeper. A colleague had an 'open door' policy and was always complaining about the pressure. When he left, he compared my secretary to Tariq Aziz, guarding my inaccessible bunker. Since this made me Saddam Hussein, I wasn't too pleased! How much better if we had explained to each other why we worked as we did, instead of coexisting in mutual disdain.

Parkinson's Law states that work expands to fill the time available – hence, the importance of allocating as much time to a task as it warrants, and no more.

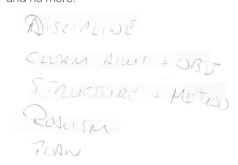
①ISCIPLINE
CLUM AIIM + OBJ
STRUCTURE + METIOD
RAULISM
PLAN

For many people, work planning needs to be linked with domestic planning.

Denlle Failures
Stm
Gail cranement
Balance g Dates
cre ven.
One latch rule
fails
Communile
Bord don all
colleagues

management techniques naïvely imagine that using these tools will ensure that everything then goes according to plan. The point is that having a plan means you become aware that you are falling behind and can do something about it sooner rather than later; at least you know where you are. Without a plan it is easy to assume that everything can still be fitted in somehow – when you should really be rescheduling, asking for help, or warning others that you cannot make a meeting. The uncertainties of organizational life make these sorts of things inevitable, from time to time. *Far from being a sign of failure, such measures may actually be a sign that you are managing your time well.*

QUESTION 2.3

What really would be signs that your work planning and time management were inadequate?

Sixth, various time-saving tips and techniques – some obvious, others rather surprising – are the final weapon in the time management armoury. These range from delegation (including delegation upwards and sideways) to slogans (such as 'do it now' and 'good enough is good') and include various ways of avoiding either wasting time or the *temptation* to waste time.

QUESTION 2.4

In what ways do the ideas of time management match the key features of the rational approach to management as described in Session 1?

Appraising time management

Does time management work? Is it a useful addition to the manager's tool-kit, a valuable set of practical, common-sense guidelines? Or is it superficial and unrealistic – perhaps even misleading and unhelpful?

ACTIVITY 2.4

Spend up to 10 minutes reviewing your experience with time management so far.

(a) Which particular ideas have you tried?

(b) What happened – what successes and difficulties did you experience?

(c) How do you explain these difficulties?

(d) Even if your success has been limited, has time management helped in *understanding* why you find it so difficult to avoid overload?

I shall ask you to look back on these notes in the next activity.

Most people find that time management is worth while and yet they also find it is far from being an answer to all of their problems with pressure and overload. In fact, people often feel decidedly ambivalent about time management: there is

obviously something in it, but somehow it does not quite deliver the goods. On the plus side, time management highlights important issues, and its core ideas can be a revelation to people new to managerial work who have become trapped in the 'fire-fighting' syndrome. For others, the gains will be less dramatic. But even so, the instruction to step back, intermittently, and think hard about your priorities and way of working is hard to fault. And most people pick up some useful ideas and pointers for saving time from the exhortations and anecdotes.

Perhaps the main problem is that time management is psychologically naïve. It works with a simple, over-rational view of management behaviour. It assumes:

- We know what we are doing – whereas situations are ambiguous: if I gossip with someone, is it time-wasting or information-gathering? Is this new project a distraction or the shape of things to come?

- We know what we want (and are realistic) – whereas our interwoven personal and organizational aims are many, subtle and constantly evolving (often it is only after the event that we realize why we took a particular course of action); and the expectations we have of ourselves may be wishful thinking.

- We are in a position to predict the outcomes of different courses of action – whereas often there is no way of knowing how long something will take, or what the consequences of not doing something might be.

- We can control our own behaviour – whereas our will-power is limited: we frequently do things that we feel like doing (for example, going to meetings) rather than the things that we know are the priority; or we take on new commitments knowing they will overload us (because it is gratifying to be busy, sought-after, important).

So, each of the assumed conditions for rational time management is problematic and, taken together, they are fairly improbable. The truth is that we are, to a greater or lesser extent, creatures of habit, and habits are hard to change. We have personal routines and 'things we have always done' which limit our willingness and ability to change our behaviour. Hence, it generally needs a crisis (such as ill health or upheavals at work) to 'unfreeze' our pattern of working or way of life and generate the commitment to change.

Advocates of time management would doubtless reply that they never said it would be easy. Determination and persistence are needed for new ways of working to become 'habits', but many people have made significant changes – often using the opportunity provided by a course that offers support and an

Life is lived forwards but only makes sense looking backwards.

There is a life and career planning exercise in Supplementary Resources: People 1. For more on the importance of a little balance, see the article 'Why executives lose their balance' by Joan Kofodimos in the *Managing Learning* course reader.

This is a bit pessimistic, surely! It seems to say to women with young children: 'Tough! You will not be able to do the job properly in a normal week.' But they can and they do.

external discipline. Indeed, far from being defensive about the limitations of their approach, some advocates of time management go further: they argue that most people simply do not carry it far enough. The fact that some people still feel overloaded and cannot fit their commitments into the time available means that they are still avoiding or are unable to make hard decisions. Usually, this is because they have not clarified their own *personal* values and priorities; they are too busy reacting to events and living up to other people's expectations. A more thorough approach involves applying broadly the same principles to *all* of one's life, not just to the time spent at work. This is sometimes called *life and career planning*. The aim is to clarify our personal values and priorities, to promote a more realistic appreciation of what we can and cannot do, and ensure a better balance between work and the other parts of our life.

But perhaps this just proves that rationalism, like any other well-worked-out set of ideas, has an answer for everything. It is a coherent, self-sealing philosophy of action. This does not mean you have to accept it.

The sceptics also have a coherent and consistent view, one that explains the appeal of time management. We like to think of ourselves as rational, purposeful and in control of things. But this is a conceit – a conceit to which time management panders. So we should not be taken in by the irrational appeal so often embedded within time management books and courses: the image of the decisive, clear-thinking manager who is in charge of events and on the road to success, while rarely working more than 40 hours a week. Life is not like that. In fact, having absorbed the ideas of time management, all the difficult judgements and hard thinking about what really matters remain; and if we still feel overloaded this does not necessarily mean that we have failed.

ACTIVITY 2.5

Where do you stand in this debate? Do your notes from Activity 2.4 suggest you identify with the rational approach, or with the criticism and reservations that have just been described? What points have I overlooked?

If you have not already worked through Chapter 6 'Managing time at work' in *The MBA Handbook*, do so now.

2.5 Conclusions

Managers work in an incredibly varied range of organizations producing all kinds of goods and services. On the face of it, their activities can have nothing in common. Nevertheless, the same characteristics of managerial work crop up again and again. And so do the traps and pitfalls that managers face in coping with their generally unbounded jobs: the danger of superficiality, of personal disorganization under pressure, of being reactive rather than proactive, of stress, and of overcommitment to the job, leading to an unbalanced life.

These are not the sorts of pitfalls that can be avoided easily or permanently, least of all through the use of neat techniques. But an awareness and understanding of the dangers is an important first step in protecting yourself and others. The ideas of time management provide part of that protection. We all need to practise them in some way, even if they have their limitations and can be misused. Time management may be easier for some people than others but we can all gain by considering its key prescriptions. In these respects, time management exemplifies the strengths and weaknesses of rational approaches in general: it offers something important but the benefits may not be achieved easily and it does not resolve completely or forever the difficulties associated with the aspects of management it addresses.

Objectives

After studying this session you should be able to:

- Distinguish between the rational and bounded rationality models of decision-making and recognize occasions when the behaviour depicted by each may be appropriate.

- Recognize the importance of the distinction between effectiveness and success in management, and the dilemma this may involve for yourself and others.

- Review your own way of working in terms of the following pitfalls: superficiality, reactivity, personal disorganization, stress and life imbalance.

- Explain briefly in your own words and with examples from your own experience the key ideas and practices associated with time management, and critically appraise its relevance for yourself and others.

SESSION 3 THE COMPLEXITIES OF MANAGEMENT

Contents

3.1 Introduction

Management courses – this one included – preach the virtues of clear objectives, clearly defined tasks, clear roles and clear lines of authority and responsibility. But often it is hard to be clear about these things – let alone to agree them with others. Any clarity we do achieve soon starts to blur in the face of new developments, new information or new ideas. Hence, for much of the time we face a degree of looseness, uncertainty, tension and even inconsistency in our activities. Indeed, there is an argument that the pursuit of clarity can be distracting or divisive. Sometimes we are not clear until after the event about what we were trying to do or our reason for doing it. And sometimes, if we *are* clear, agreement is impossible – papering over the cracks can be a useful expedient.

This session is about understanding the various uncertainties and complexities that managers face. Managerial work can be seen as complicated in two ways.

First, *being* a manager can be complicated. Some aspects of this personal, 'internal' complexity have already been considered in the discussion of the pressures and stresses of managerial work in Session 2. I shall explore this issue a little further here, this time in terms of the *roles* you take on as a manager. *When we understand our role, appropriate conduct follows*. Moreover, thinking in terms of roles provides a way of making sense of many of the tensions and uncertainties – even if sometimes you still cannot do anything much about them. These topics take up the first half of this session.

Second, there is the 'external', more impersonal complexity that it is a manager's job to address – the complications a manager has to deal with on a daily basis. Considering the different sorts of problems that managers face leads to some useful distinctions, and to the loose-knit body of ideas and approaches associated with 'systems thinking' of one sort or another. Love them or hate them, organizational life is permeated by systems, and systems ideas provide some useful tools for coping with complexity. These topics take up the second half of this session.

The aims of this session are to:

- Explore further the tensions, uncertainties and dilemmas experienced by managers.

- Show that a 'roles' perspective can illuminate some of those tensions, uncertainties and dilemmas.

- Present another view of managerial work as primarily a matter of problem-solving.

- Prepare for later parts of the course by introducing some of the main ideas and concerns associated with the use of systems terminology.

3.2 Understanding management roles

The idea of role is probably already familiar to you – the phrase 'wearing my other hat' is a cliché, after all. But it is important to understand the two main ways in which the term 'role' is used. It may refer to a particular organizational *position* (for example, area manager, project leader), involving a set of rights and responsibilities. It also refers to *the part we play* in a given situation ('let me play devil's advocate for a moment ...') but, as we shall see, not all such 'parts' are expressed explicitly. *In practice*, these two uses of the concept – one structural and one from a theatrical metaphor – tend to run together, simply because most positions need to be improvised; they are not exhaustively detailed and fixed forever. So the term 'role' can be defined as *the set of expectations held by the person concerned and by those he or she interacts with about the appropriate contribution he or she will make in a given situation.*

Using the term in this way, I shall talk both about your role as a manager – the 'overall' role that links what would otherwise be disparate experiences at work – and about the roles that you need to take up, or find yourself playing, at particular moments as part of that overall management role. The formal way of saying this is that a manager's *role-set* contains several different roles (see Figure 3.1).

There is an example of an analysis of management roles in Box 3.1 (overleaf). It is drawn from one of the studies of managerial work considered in Session 2. Many people find that this set of roles captures the experience of management rather well, but there is nothing sacrosanct about it.

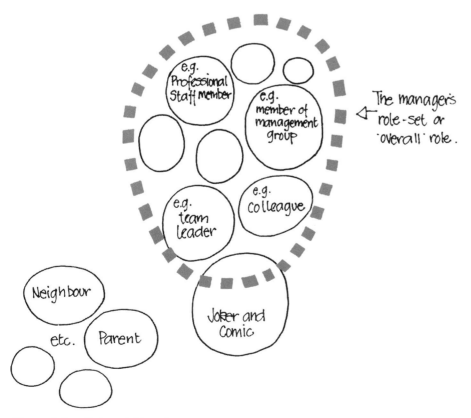

Figure 3.1   *Roles within roles*

Box 3.1   Mintzberg on a manager's roles

Mintzberg suggests that there are ten managerial roles, which can be grouped into three areas: *interpersonal, informational* and *decisional.* Interpersonal roles cover the relationships that a manager has to have with others. The three roles within this category are figurehead, leader and liaison. Managers have to act as *figureheads* because of their formal authority and symbolic position, representing their organizations. As *leaders*, managers have to bring together the needs of an organization and those of the individuals under their command. The third interpersonal role, that of *liaison*, deals with the horizontal relationships which work-activity studies have shown to be important for a manager. A manager has to maintain a network of relationships outside the organization.

Managers have to collect, disseminate and transmit information and have three corresponding informational roles, namely monitor, disseminator and spokesman [*sic*]. A manager is an important figure in *monitoring* what goes on in the organization, receiving information about both internal and external events, and transmitting it to others. This process of transmission is the *dissemination* role, passing on information of both a factual and value kind. A manager often has to give information concerning the organization to outsiders, taking on the role of *spokesman* to both the general public and those in positions of influence.

As with so many writers about management, Mintzberg regards the most crucial part of managerial activity as that concerned with making decisions. The four roles that he places in this category are based on different classes of decision, namely, entrepreneur, disturbance handler, resource allocator and negotiator. As *entrepreneurs*, managers make decisions about changing what is happening in an organization. They may have to both initiate change and to take an active part in deciding exactly what is to be done. In principle, they are acting voluntarily. This is very different from their role as a *disturbance handler*, where managers have to make decisions which arise from events beyond their control and unpredicted. The ability to react to events as well as to plan activities is an important managerial skill in Mintzberg's eyes.

The *resource allocation* role of a manager is central to much organizational analysis. Clearly a manager has to make decisions about the allocation of money, people, equipment, time and so on. Mintzberg points out that in doing so a manager is actually scheduling time, programming work and authorizing actions. The *negotiation* role is put in the decisional category by Mintzberg because it is 'resource trading in real time'. A manager has to negotiate with others and in the process be able to make decisions about the commitment of organizational resources.

For Mintzberg these ten roles provide a more adequate description of what managers do than any of the various schools of management thought. In these roles it is information that is crucial; the manager is determining the priority of information. Through the interpersonal roles a manager acquires information, and through the decisional roles it is put into use.

The scope for each manager to choose a different blend of roles means that management is not reducible to a set of scientific statements and programmes. Management is essentially an art and it is necessary for managers to try to learn continuously about their own situations.

(Source: Pugh and Hickson, 1989, pp. 32–3)

ACTIVITY 3.1

Spend 10 minutes analysing your own managerial activity in terms of
Mintzberg's 10 roles. Start by noting examples of things you do that would fall
within each of the roles described. You may find it helpful to go through your
job description and your Activity Log, placing the various responsibilities and
activities under one or more roles.

Interpersonal roles

- figurehead
- leader
- liaison

Informational roles

- monitoring
- dissemination
- spokesperson

Decisional roles

- entrepreneur
- disturbance handler
- resource allocator
- negotiator

Now write brief answers to the following questions.

(a) Which roles are important and which are unimportant in your job?
     You might give them each two, one or no asterisks.

(b) With which roles are you *most* and *least* comfortable?

(c) Does the range of your roles throw any light on the problems of
     managing your time, such as the difficulty of delegating or of saying 'no'
     to particular tasks? Would it be helpful to think in terms of avoiding or
     passing on certain *roles* (rather than tasks)?

*It takes a bit of effort to get used to seeing things Mintzberg's way. However,
many people find that this set of roles captures the experience of management
rather well. If you found this approach illuminating you might like to rewrite your
job description in terms of Mintzberg's roles.*

Sources of role

The roles that people play in organizations are shaped by the three different
'pulls' shown in Figure 3.2 (overleaf). I shall consider each of these pulls in turn.

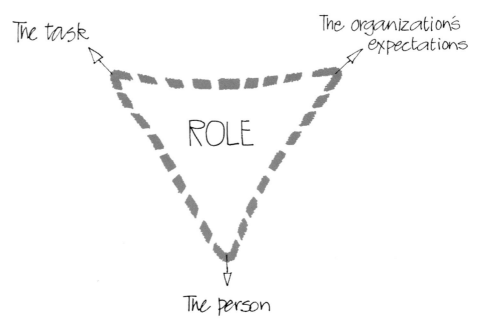

Figure 3.2 *Sources of role*

Task and role

An organization's tasks have their own logic or momentum and create unanticipated demands on staff and managers. Hence, managers who have been 'tasked' with a particular piece of work may have to drop everything in order to 'keep the show on the road'. This is most obvious in the case of project managers whose working lives can be completely dominated by major project deadlines or events. Commitment to the task or project can then come into conflict with a commitment to the organization which has defined the manager's role in a particular way. For example, a central part of the job of one senior manager I know is to negotiate development plans with the 20 or more local offices in her region. These plans are agreed annually and for various reasons, concerning both the availability of information and the timing of policy directives, the visits that finalize and document these agreed plans have to take place in a six to eight week period towards the end of the financial year. Done casually, such plans are bland bureaucratic formalities. Done properly, with considerable preparation and a proper record kept of the discussions, agreeing these plans is immensely worth while for all involved. The problem is that for six to eight weeks this task completely dominates the work of my friend and others in her position. Yet, during this time, the organization still expects her to carry out her role in the normal way – attending policy working groups, joining in divisional meetings, representing the organization externally, and so on. This brings us to the next pull on a manager's role.

Organization and role

In general, *how* managers carry out their roles, the demands they experience, the constraints they face, and the choices they make are all conditioned by the expectations that others have of them. Many of these expectations can never appear in job descriptions or policy statements but their impact is none the less powerful. For example, senior managers appointed with a brief to introduce certain changes are often surprised at the obstacles they feel are put in their way by the very people who appointed them to 'get things moving'. The term *role ambiguity* is often used to refer to situations involving uncertainty about what is expected of a person in a particular role. Most of us have experienced this, especially when starting a new job.

Another set of problems concerns the tensions that can arise between the expectations that different people have of the same manager. This is often referred to as *role conflict*. For example, when hard decisions have to be made the staff and managers below you may expect you to represent their views to the 'upper echelons' (Mintzberg's 'spokesman' role). But as a manager you are also expected to be loyal to the organization in presenting its policies and decisions to your staff (the 'leadership' and 'dissemination' roles). The temptation is to side with staff when with staff and to side with senior management when with senior management – whereas the reverse position, although uncomfortable, may be what is really required.

HE TAKES HIS DIFFERENT ROLES VERY SERIOUSLY

Person and role

What kind of person you are influences the way in which you take up a role and the kind of role you take up. Some people find it easy enough to give orders; others are happier to work through consensus. Some people are at their best in a crisis; others generally prefer an ordered life.

The fact that who you are shines through the roles you take up is inevitable. Whether it works for or against you, and for or against your organization, depends on the situation. When your experiences, aptitudes and values match the requirements and expectations of the job, you will carry out the role with confidence and satisfaction. You will be 'doing what comes naturally'. On the other hand, when you are expected to be and do things that, in varying degrees, clash with your experience, aptitudes and inclinations, you are likely to encounter difficulties and tensions. For example, an organization may expect people to work in a particular way, and they may endorse this and claim to be doing so because they like to imagine themselves as that sort of person; but in reality they are not like that. All human beings have an underestimated capacity for self-deception – and managers are no exception. I may espouse accountability to a steering committee – but to others it is obvious that I try to preserve my autonomy and stay in control. Or I may like to think of myself as the sort of decisive manager that the organization favours – but actually I find it hard to make decisions, especially when the more assertive members of my staff disagree among themselves on what should be done.

So, there is also a psychological dimension to managing and management. Indeed, it is a truism that staff relate to their managers as authority figures, both actually and symbolically. Much of the suspicion of management stems from feelings people have about authority, and especially the fear that 'authority' will be 'authoritarian'. Indeed, for some people, 'authority' may *mean* 'authoritarian'. This is not a trivial matter. Historically, management has often been authoritarian. Tell many people that they are 'in charge' and they presume that they have to control other people. What is more, these other people will probably expect to be told what to do (whether or not this is happening). Such expectations can lie under the surface, even in organizations that try to work in teams and on the basis of empowerment. Our feelings about authority (and leaders and managers) show up in all kinds of ways. In some organizations the positive and negative aspects of management are shared out. A 'benign' manager or director is widely appreciated because there is someone else, often a financial manager, who is seen to take unpopular decisions. Box 3.2 provides a psychologist's view of these issues.

Box 3.2   Becoming a manager

The [manager] 'inherits' each group member's 'inner child of the past'. For each of us has a past history of being a child, intimately involved in multiple relationships with a variety of adults: parents, grandparents, schoolteachers, coaches, scout leaders, piano teachers, school principals, and of course the infamous assistant principal. All these adults had power and authority over us when we were youngsters, and most of them used it frequently. All children try out different behaviours to cope with these 'authority figures'. Some of their coping mechanisms prove effective, some ineffective. Those that work get used again and again, and so become habitual responses to all other adults who try to control and dominate them.

These coping mechanisms are seldom discarded when children pass into adolescence, or when they enter adulthood. They remain an integral part of the adult personality, to be called upon (or unconsciously triggered) whenever she or he enters a relationship with someone holding power or authority. So all adults in a very real sense harbour an 'inner child of the past' that will strongly influence how they react to leaders.

When thrust into each new relationship with an authority figure, people naturally employ those same coping mechanisms that were built in by habitual use throughout their lifetime. This is why a leader inherits the inner child of the past of each of his or her group members.

(Source: Gordon, 1977)

QUESTION 3.1

The extract in Box 3.2 describes how, when staff react to a manager as an authority figure, their behaviour may be affected by ways of relating that developed in their formative years. How else may the interaction between manager and subordinates be distorted by the residue of childhood experiences?

Prejudice, lack of confidence, over reliance on authority

ACTIVITY 3.2

Try to note down an occasion from your own experience that illustrates each of the following behaviours.

	By you	By others
Behaviour carrying an authoritarian impulse	*Dining*	*Sone*
Behaviour carrying a submissive *or* rebellious impulse	*So'Kan*	*Neunplien*

You probably found it easier to think of examples of other people's behaviour than of your own. Most of us are only half-aware of these dimensions of our conduct, and often not even that. Sometimes it is easier to recognize these elements in events that happened a while ago. On the other hand, if the 'by others' behaviour related to you, the same situation may also illustrate a 'by you' behaviour. Roles always tend to become complementary.

The emotional 'under-life' of organizations

Organizations have a rich emotional life – they are not just impersonal instruments of some dispassionate purpose. Organizations meet, or fail to meet, the psychological needs of those involved in ways that are not always explicit or intended. We all have these needs and if they are not met we find ways of objecting, of being ineffective, even of sabotaging our own work (the 'being your own worst enemy' syndrome). How you undertake your role will be in part an expression of or a response to those emotional currents: a way of expressing your own needs and responding to others' needs.

This emotional 'under-life' of organizations does not just concern authority. For example, a common anxiety at work is the feeling of not being as effective as one would like to be. Then there are all the anxieties about how one is viewed by others, and about one's prospects and security within the organization. In addition, the work of many organizations, particularly statutory and non-profit agencies, evokes strong feelings. Where staff are exposed to physical strain, to danger, to abuse, to human suffering, or to clients who are very demanding because of illness or disadvantage, they too may experience strong feelings. They may become angry and resentful, which can show up in criticism of others even when this criticism is inappropriate. The manager can become a convenient receptacle for all these negative feelings, and it is a management task to acknowledge the uncertainties, anxieties and distress, and to arrange the work so that those involved are supported.

This is not part of management as some understand it, but the problems do not go away if they are ignored, as the 'decisive manager' syndrome illustrates. 'Decisive managers' think of management in only a mechanical or functional way, as a number of tasks. Managers who take this approach give a down-to-earth impression of getting things done, are irritated by the time-wasting tactics of those who want to 'discuss the issues', and often express an antipathy to meetings. 'I'm not interested in problems, only solutions' is the message, whether or not it is said explicitly.

Moreover, the decisive manager behaves in a way that seems to confirm that impression of efficiency; inefficiency in the system has to be located elsewhere. By taking a strong position, others are put at a disadvantage, and are reluctant to appear hesitant, negative or slow on the uptake. The decisive manager's staff in particular are likely to be drawn into dependent ('hidden child of the past') responses. Likewise, when problems arise, the decisive manager is quick to imply that the blame lies elsewhere (even if he or she has been in too much of a hurry to think through a course of action, or explain properly what needed to be done).

This confirms the manager's view of his or her competence and others' incompetence. Inadequate work may be justified by claiming a peculiarly rigid notion of time management as a virtue. When dilemmas cannot be ignored, it will be because some other group or person has not made up their mind and stated what the objectives should be.

Working with this kind of manager is not easy: they are, in effect, *passing on their own uncertainty and anxiety* – which only adds to the difficulties of others. Too much (apparent) certainty is often associated with insensitivity and inflexibility in other respects. Such managers may believe that the activity for which they are responsible is self-evidently efficient and worth while, even if it has become self-serving and bears little relation to what is required. These managers are then failing their organizations, which may in turn lose confidence in them. Senior figures may start asking what they are really getting for the resources tied up in that area.

The general point, then, is that to ignore the ambiguities and uncertainties of management both imposes on colleagues and undermines performance. We need to be able to accommodate doubts, recognize our mistakes and live with criticism – this is 'negative capability', to use a phrase by the poet Keats (see Box 3.3).

Box 3.3   Charles Handy on negative capability

Keats defined 'negative capability' in his letters in 1817 as 'when a man is capable of being in uncertainties, mysteries, and doubts'. I would extend the meaning to include the capacity to live with mistakes and failures without being downhearted or dismayed.

We will never know enough about that unknown to be certain of the result. We will get it wrong some of the time. Doubt and mistakes must not be allowed to disturb us because it is from them that we learn ...

Entrepreneurs, the successful ones, have on average nine failures for every success. It is only the successes that you will hear about, the failures they credit to experience. Oil companies expect to drill nine empty wells for every one that flows. Getting it wrong is part of getting it right ... Negative capability is an attitude of mind which learners need to cultivate, to help them to write off their mistakes as experience. It helps to get your first failures early on; the later ones are then less painful. Those who have a gilded youth, in which success leads on to success, are sometimes the least experimental and the most conservative as they grow older because the fear of failure looms larger ...

We learn by our mistakes, as we always tell ourselves, not from our successes; but perhaps we do not really believe it. We should, for we change by exploration not by retracing well-known paths. We start our learning with uncertainties and doubts, with questions to be resolved.

We grow older wondering who we will be and what we will do. For organizations as for individuals life is a book still to be written. If we cannot live with these uncertainties we will not learn and change will always be an unpleasant surprise.

(Source: Handy, 1991, pp. 54–6)

So, how can you constructively manage the emotional 'under-life' of the organization – as it is reflected in your own anxieties and needs as well as in other people's? And how can the roles perspective help make sense of the normal confusions of organizational life?

Clearly, this is not the sort of issue that has pat answers or can be tackled with a particular technique. In the most general terms, what is needed is *awareness* and *understanding*. It is a matter of learning to recognize particular signs and having the frameworks to make sense of them. What does all this mean, more specifically? First, your own feelings about your activities become data for understanding your role. This is why some of the earlier activities asked you to consider your feelings about different aspects of your role: they are clues to what is going on.

Our feelings also warn us when we are in danger of *slipping out of role* and behaving inappropriately. For example, if you are eager for someone's friendship and support you may be tempted to ingratiate yourself by being over-friendly, or by making indiscreet comments about your organization or the people in it. Such behaviour is incompatible with your role and is likely to confuse the other person, especially when you go back into role and behave like a manager again. In general, strong feelings – such as anger – can easily draw us out of our roles. This does *not* mean that in your managerial role you have to be emotionally neutral. You can still be angry (or friendly, needy, and so on) *in* role – that is to say, in ways that are appropriate to your work and situation. You will be much better able to stay in role if you recognize these feelings.

This is often a problem for managers who feel isolated in their role (and it is a sign that they must seek support elsewhere if it is unavailable within the organization).

Secondly, all role relationships are negotiated, and are open to further negotiation. This negotiation of roles is crucial to effective management. It is important to be clear that 'negotiation' does not necessarily or usually mean explicit across-the-table negotiation. This sort of negotiation is implicit, is usually not examined, and is conducted through successive understandings and misunderstandings about the nature of the relationship or the task.

For example, a regional manager is invited to a discussion at head office. She sees herself as contributing the views of regional managers to the formulation of new guidelines; she expects to be in spokesperson and negotiator roles. But the meeting is difficult. The guidelines seem to have already been decided and the discussion is only to obtain her ideas on the implementation difficulties and to consider how best to present the guidelines to other regional managers. In other words, the head office managers see her purely in her dissemination role, as an agent more than a colleague, and relate to her accordingly.

For this reason the discussion starts off rather at cross-purposes, as the regional manager tries to get the others to respond to her appropriately in her role as she sees it. During the meeting this implicit negotiation of her role could develop in different ways. She may insist on her representational and negotiation roles, but not have them accepted by others. Then she may refuse to accept the *fait accompli* and, either openly or covertly, refuse to take up the subordinate disseminator role expected of her. Or she may gradually slip into that role (and perhaps feel frustrated and ineffective). Or she may hold on to the representational role and win some acceptance of it while accepting that she also needs to operate in other capacities as well. (I am not concerned here with the 'right' outcome – only to illustrate the *idea* of tacit role negotiation.)

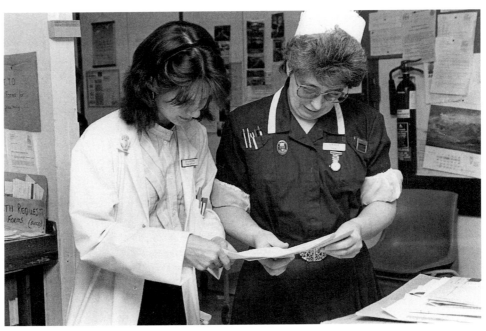

You may have a dual role to play, both as a specialist and as a manager

Thirdly, by reflecting on the roles you take up or find yourself in, you will become more familiar with the role perspective and be more readily able to pinpoint the roles. It may then be helpful to share and test your perceptions against those of others in a more explicit way: for example, 'I seem to be taking on the role of "loyal opposition" in relation to these proposals. Is that OK with you?'; or 'I feel I'm being cast in the role of "go-between" in these negotiations. How does it look to you?'. You will find that the language of roles is a useful way of communicating your view of a relationship and opening up a discussion of what is bothering each side.

Finally, it is part of a manager's role to recognize and acknowledge the feelings of staff and colleagues – both out of respect for them and because otherwise the organization's work will suffer. It does not necessarily follow that you will then have to 'do something' to prevent the feelings recurring – that will often be quite impossible. (If you do feel that way, what does it say about how you have been interpreting your role?) Nor does it mean wallowing in anxiety or despair – the work must continue. The manager's role in this respect is better understood in terms of *containment* – neither dismissing nor reinforcing the feelings but providing a safe setting in which they can be expressed. In this way the feelings can often be put aside and they are much less likely to build up or to emerge in dysfunctional ways.

The archetype of this role is the containment of a child's intense anxieties by a parent. By accepting the child's feelings, which may at times be aggressive and hateful as well as loving, parents give the child the opportunity to learn to live with their anxieties and become confident that it is possible to survive feelings of anger, loss and despair. So not all 'parental' roles are to be avoided in management (even if we could do so).

A similar point can be made about apparently 'childish' roles: they too have their positive contribution (for example, in creative problem-solving, where many techniques are based on triggering the naïve child within, and in contributing enthusiasm or humour to activities). This is worth remembering if you are beginning to feel that people only mean problems. The emotional 'under-life' of most organizations has currents of warmth, joy and excitement as well as anxiety and hostility.

ACTIVITY 3.3

Consider carefully two instances when you felt perplexed, angry, anxious, frustrated, depressed or overwhelmed. (Your notes for Activities 2.1 and 3.1, where you noted aspects of your work and roles with which you are and are not comfortable, may be relevant.)

(a) What do the feelings suggest about how the role you were carrying out related to the task or was received by other people?

(b) Given essentially the same situation, can you imagine adjustments in your understanding and conduct of the role and/or the tasks required and/or the expectations of others which would have allowed you to perform your role somewhat more comfortably and competently? What would these adjustments be?

(c) With hindsight, can you see ways in which, before or during the incidents you are considering, you could have negotiated a rather different role that might have reduced the difficulties?

Your answers to questions (b) and (c) may have been quite definitely 'No'. Not all difficulties can be avoided and, when they cannot, we have to handle the feelings that arise.

3.3 The management of complexity

Another answer to the question 'What do managers do?' is that they spend their working lives continually diagnosing problems and working out how to solve them. In some ways, they are like doctors in general practice – they may not solve a particular problem themselves but they know someone who can, or they can deal with some aspects of it. Whether you agree that problem-solving is the essence of managerial work, it is certainly an important role. So what does it involve? And what are the implications for managers?

Two sorts of problems, two sorts of complexity

Problems vary enormously in their complexity and seriousness. They range from minor upsets through to near-catastrophes, from temporary hitches to persistent, gnawing 'tangles'. So it will help to introduce a distinction: I shall refer to simpler, more limited sorts of problems as 'difficulties', and the nastier, more taxing ones as 'messy problems' or just 'messes'. The reasons for making this distinction will soon become clear but, in essence, messes are not just 'bigger' than difficulties: they have several features that make them qualitatively different. As a result, the sorts of activities needed to tackle these two sorts of problems can be very different.

ACTIVITY 3.4

This activity will help you to think critically about the material that follows in relation to your own experience. You should spend about 15 minutes on this first stage of the exercise. (You will need to return to your notes for other activities later in this session.)

(a) Note down at least three difficulties you have faced recently in your organization. Then note down three (or more) of the biggest and messiest problems you have ever faced or been involved in tackling.

(b) List the ways in which the difficulties and the messes differ. What are the characteristics of the major, nagging problems that distinguish them from the more limited ones? You should aim for a list of at least six points.

Although everyone expresses the differences between difficulties and messes in their own terms, the distinguishing features that people come up with can usually be grouped under one of two headings. The first concerns the scale of the problem and covers all the ways in which messy problems tend to be 'larger' than difficulties. Thus, messy problems usually have more serious implications and people are much more likely to worry about them. More people are likely to be involved. A mess covers a larger area; it includes several interlocking aspects and it may appear in a number of different guises. Messy problems usually have a longer time-scale. They tend to haunt the people affected for months, or even years. Messy problems are more difficult to tackle; they are more complicated. All of these are ways in which messes can usually be distinguished from difficulties.

However, for most people, these factors, although essential, do not capture some crucial features that make messes really troublesome. The second group of key features comes under the general heading of uncertainty: with messes there is much more about which one is simply unsure. In fact, this uncertainty starts with the problem itself: a difficulty is fairly clear cut, it is quite easy to put a label on it, or to explain it to someone else. But a messy problem is hard to pin down; it is difficult to say what the problem is and yet things are not right. With a difficulty I know roughly what a solution will look like; with a mess, I am not at all sure. Indeed, with a mess it may not make much sense to talk about 'a solution'. It may be a matter of coping with the circumstances as best as one can. With a difficulty I can take for granted the overall context and purpose of the activity; it is simply a matter of how it can best be done. But a messy problem calls into question my priorities and assumptions; I am not sure how much weight to give to different considerations, whether particular goals are realistic or should be abandoned. Moreover, with a mess, more aspects are beyond my direct control.

With a difficulty I know which factors are part of the problem or relevant to it and which are not; I can disentangle it from the broader context of my work and address it as a more or less discrete matter. But a messy problem is 'fuzzy'; it is hard to say who and what is involved in the problem and who and what is not, because the different elements are closely tied to other areas of activity in the organization. Finally, with a difficulty I either know enough to tackle it or I know what I need to know; with a mess I do not know enough and I am uncertain even of what I need to know. Features of this sort are characteristic of messy problems and generate a distinctive quality of uncertainty, of 'not knowing' and, hence, of unease when one faces them.

In practice, the factors that contribute to the scale of the problem and those that contribute to the uncertainty associated with it are hard to separate. More extensive problems will usually also be less clear cut. Not knowing how serious a problem is can itself be considered rather a serious matter. The more people

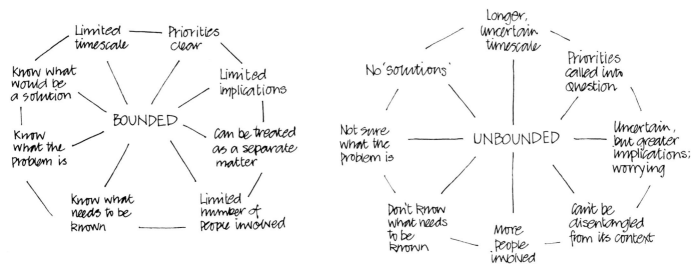

Figure 3.3   *Difficulties: characteristically smaller and well defined*

Figure 3.4   *Messy problems: characteristically bigger and poorly defined*

involved, the more likely it is that the problem will be inseparable from much other organizational work and raise questions about goals and priorities.

One idea captures the differences of both scale and uncertainty: the idea that difficulties are bounded while messes are unbounded. Saying that a problem is bounded implies not just that it is fairly limited but that one knows roughly where those limits are. By contrast, an unbounded problem is more extensive but quite how extensive one cannot say. Most of the qualities of difficulties and messes referred to above clearly relate to the bounded/unbounded distinction. Figures 3.3 and 3.4 summarize these points, the attributes of difficulties being shown as aspects of 'boundedness' and the attributes of messes as aspects of 'unboundedness'.

ACTIVITY 3.5

Compare your notes on the differences between difficulties and messes with those given in the text.

(a) Do the characteristics shown in Figure 3.3 add to, or help you clarify, your understanding of what constitute your 'big, complicated problems'? Or does my discussion miss essential aspects of the circumstances you find demanding and troublesome?

(b) Can you now think of other problems you have faced or have been involved with that are better examples of the sorts of problems I call messes? Can you think of occasions when you have mistaken a mess for a difficulty, and vice versa? How do you account for your mistake?

You can explore the idea of messy problems in more detail in the short, lively article by Russ Ackoff, 'The art and science of mess management', in the *Managing Change* course reader.

The distinction between difficulties and messes leads to another important distinction – between two different sorts of complexity. Complexity is not just a matter of there being many different factors and interactions to bear in mind, of uncertainty concerning some of them, or of a multitude of combinations and permutations of possible decisions and events to allow for, evaluate and select. It is not only a computational matter. Complexity is also generated by the very different interpretations that can be placed on those factors, decisions and events.

The first type of complexity, which generates difficult computational problems, I shall call *hard complexity* and illustrate by the game of chess. With up to 16 pieces on each side at any one time, each one capable of many moves, the range of possibilities is clearly enormous: a vast number of move and countermove sequences may have to be considered and assessed. It is, unquestionably, complicated. Nevertheless, the nature of the game, the moves of the pieces, the fundamental purposes of the players – all these are unproblematic.

By contrast, consider the situation in a detective story at the end of the penultimate chapter, when the hero is about to unravel the mystery. Once again, the situation is complicated but in a quite different way. Usually, the number of possible murderers is quite limited – perhaps only half a dozen. So, on the face of it, choosing among them should be a fairly manageable task. But, in this case, the complexity arises not from the 'facts' but from the variety of quite different constructions that can be put on them. The information the author has given you may, in principle, be sufficient but it is incomplete. It also contains much that will prove quite irrelevant or misleading.

If several people read the novel each will, before the final unravelling, have different hunches about who did what, how and why. The complexity, and the fascination, of such stories lies in the tantalising multiplicity of interpretations and reconstructions that are possible. The description of events is ambiguous, and deliberately so. I shall call this sort of complexity *soft complexity*.

Chess, with its complicated calculations, and detective novels that are complicated because of extreme ambiguity are a long way from the world of management, so an illustration of hard and soft complexity in an organizational context is also needed.

The reorganization of a hospital's waste-disposal arrangements is a fairly messy problem. In the UK, hospitals can be prosecuted for failing to meet strict safety and environmental legislation, including the requirement that clinical waste be burned at a temperature in excess of 1000°C. Consider the case of Nightingale General in Box 3.4 (opposite).

Most hospitals in the UK are publicly funded and the state of the National Health Service is often a political issue.

The point about the Nightingale General case is that it is not clear which are the relevant variables in calculating likely costs and benefits, given the vast number of variables that might, in principle, be considered. Or rather, it is clear that there will be no agreement on which are the relevant factors. Radically different conceptions of the problems and possibilities are involved; even if these could, in principle, be resolved by lengthy comparative experiments – which is by no means certain given the interests and values involved – such experiments are unlikely to be a practical possibility. So the problem has to be considered within incompatible frames of reference; the different interpretations cannot simply be added together.

Such a situation involves soft complexity – at least for the hospital managers as a group, if not for particular individuals within the group. Some of the people involved could be unwilling to recognize alternative constructions of the issues, or will consider them too fanciful to merit serious consideration. And if everyone adopts such a position there can be no dialogue, only a power struggle, pure and simple. More commonly, although people do press particular interpretations and the political dimension is ever-present, they also recognize that other views exist and that there may be something in them. Even if they start with a clear idea of the problem, they may become uncertain about what the issues really are, or about the best terms in which to consider them.

Box 3.4   Waste disposal at Nightingale General

Previously, all waste at Nightingale General was burned, unsorted, in the old incinerator which operated at 400° C, but it is now clear to the hospital's managers that a new, and very expensive, incinerator must be bought to comply with new legislation. There are genuinely difficult issues surrounding the appropriate choice of incinerator. Should it completely replace the existing plant and continue to burn unsorted waste as before? There are clearly trade-offs between the long-term and short-term advantages and disadvantages, not least that the high-temperature incinerator is expensive to run. Should the old incinerator be retained to burn non-clinical waste and a much smaller clinical-waste incinerator be built as an additional facility?

These options must be addressed by a painstaking examination of the various factors associated with each one. This is hard complexity. But at any point in considering such a problem the examination of possibilities may expose conflicting aspirations and assumptions about the equipment that cannot be resolved by reference to agreed 'facts' or estimates. Some of the people involved may want to redefine the problem, introducing quite different classes of solution that cannot be strictly compared with those considered so far. For example, this may be seen as an opportunity to increase the hospital's revenue by providing an incineration service for neighbouring hospitals, clinics and general practitioners (family doctors). This view points towards some complicated issues concerning the optimum level of investment and the redefinition of hospital goals. It may make sense to separate entrepreneurial activity from 'mainstream' hospital activities.

Another view would see the disposal of clinical and non-clinical waste as simply part of the overall task of hospital 'housekeeping'. Under existing arrangements, all waste is treated as clinical waste, from used stationery, packaging and dead flowers to hazardous waste. It is all treated as dangerous and is collected in yellow plastic sacks. Concerns have been expressed that handling all waste as hazardous waste increases the cost of its handling and that, since almost all of the waste 'looks normal', procedures can be sloppy. Should the collection system be modified so that waste is sorted at source and only trained personnel handle the hazardous yellow sacks? From this point of view, the key issues are training and monitoring of waste-collection practices.

A third view cuts right across the others and sees the basic problem as one of reducing the quantity of waste needing disposal. Single-use sterile packs and disposable equipment have dramatically increased the plastic and paper component of the hazardous waste. Perhaps it is time to reassess the costs of this fashion against traditional sterilization procedures.

Each of the views mentioned in the Nightingale General case can be subjected to powerful counter-arguments and protagonists could run down their opponents by speculating about their 'real' motives.

All of this must be considered against a background in which it is politically sensitive to spend money on anything other than 'patient care' and in a situation where staff at all levels feel pressured and harassed by the steadily increasing demands made of them.

Distinguishing between these two sorts of complexity further clarifies the difference between difficulties and messes. Difficulties, being well-defined and more limited problems, mainly involve hard complexity. Given a particular view of the matter, what is the best that can be done? Messy problems, on the other hand, include large measures of both hard and soft complexity. Of course this may not be obvious at first, and some or all of those involved may fail to recognize the soft complexity: they may initially resent alternative viewpoints, perhaps seeing them as misguided or even wilful attempts to confuse the 'real' issue. ('Let's deal with one thing at a time!' or 'Let's stick to the facts, for heaven's sake!') Ambiguity and different interpretations, which can be overlooked or ignored when working on your own or with close colleagues, are harder to avoid when more people are involved. People from other areas of the organization are liable to present quite different views. Other people's input will often help you see that the problem is messier than first thought. Indeed, only the most trivial difficulties involve no soft complexity at all. But the more soft complexity there is, the messier the problem is likely to be. Working out what to do with a messy problem is no longer just a matter of thinking the problem through but of *re*thinking the problem as well.

In general, tackling messy problems involves sharing, challenging and reformulating different interpretations of 'the problem'. It is a process of articulating and clarifying differences, of gathering information through the co-operation of others, of negotiating agreement and cultivating commitment for a course of action. It literally makes no sense to say, 'I had the solution, but they wouldn't listen.' Hence, tackling messy problems is simultaneously an analytical and a social process. An answer that lacks organizational backing is no answer at all. Of course, there are occasions when orders are given and have to be accepted; but generally, where messy problems are concerned, there is a progression from initial individual and conflicting interpretations through to an agreement, albeit limited and provisional, on what is to be done and how. If this social process does not happen, neither will the solution – or it will be watered down, diverted and rendered ineffective.

One final point about the difference between hard and soft complexity is very important. Particular methods, approaches and academic disciplines have developed to tackle mainly hard complexity in different contexts. The same is true for soft complexity. Hence, we can distinguish, at least in broad terms, between hard and soft approaches, disciplines and ways of thinking. In general, people with a scientific, an engineering or a financial background will tend (at least initially) to recognize and respond to the elements of hard complexity in a particular situation; people with an arts, a social science, a legal or a human relations background will recognize and respond to the elements of soft complexity. We see what we have been trained to see – but every way of seeing is also a way of not seeing. Although hard and soft approaches are both important and are complementary, these different ways of thinking run deep; collaboration between people who have each been steeped in only one approach is seldom easy. Technologists often become impatient with conflicting views and concerns and want to get on with the business; 'people' people, on the other hand, are often intimidated by numbers and calculations and secretly hope they will not really matter. Hence, being able to recognize and deal with both sorts of complexity is essential for anyone who wants to earn a living tackling messy problems.

QUESTION 3.2

Which of the following cases involve primarily hard complexity and which involve primarily soft complexity? Briefly explain your choice in each case.

(a) A betting agent wondering whether to adjust the odds on offer.

Probably – HARD

(b) A historian trying to account for particular social changes.

Soft – Conjecture, as amp—

(c) An insurance underwriter trying to decide rates for motor insurance.

Hard – Probability experience model based on historical data

(d) An engineer choosing between different possible designs for a bridge.

Hard Soft – aesthetics

(e) A planner deciding how big a bridge is needed and where it should be located.

Hard –

ACTIVITY 3.6

In the light of the discussion of hard and soft complexity, spend five minutes reviewing your notes on the messy problems you have faced.

(a) What are the elements of both hard and soft complexity in the problems?

(b) In what ways does the discussion of soft complexity help in pinning down what for you distinguished the messes from the difficulties?

(c) If you have been thinking about the messy problems in terms of either hard complexity or soft complexity, how do you account for this: in terms of your particular work, or your particular training and way of thinking?

(d) Do you see yourself as a 'hard' or a 'soft' thinker, or as a bit of both? Do you attend more to the analytical or the social dimensions of the process of working on messy problems? What are the implications for your management learning?

Systems, complexity and management

The twentieth century saw an explosion of knowledge and theorizing. Established fields have been transformed and entirely new disciplines have emerged. One obvious result of this has been the proliferation of new specialisms and an ever-wider and more diverse range of knowledge-based occupations. Through all this upheaval and rapid development one concept – the idea of the *system* – has been a recurring motif. It has been associated with new approaches and ideas in theoretical as well as applied fields, and in the physical as well as the social sciences. Indeed, since the 1950s it has become a part of everyday language.

The various theoretical, technical and vernacular usages of the term 'system' have important differences. The common thread is that 'system' is a way of referring to some sort of *organized complexity*. The term is used to refer to (and can be defined as) a *functioning configuration of interrelated elements*. Such configurations may be very concrete (for example, an assembly line) or entirely abstract (for example, a *system of ideas*, which provides a way of interpreting information and events).

The various systems approaches or methods that have appeared in different fields are essentially ways of analysing, or designing, or deciding about, complicated phenomena, technologies or situations. Box 3.5 summarizes some of the fields in and around management that have used and developed systems ideas, thereby importing them into management thinking and practice.

Box 3.5 Systems ideas and approaches relevant to management

Operations research and systems thinking

This was originally a matter of scientists and applied mathematicians building and using quantitative models to improve decision-making. This work still continues, and it has generated a family of analytic tools – linear programming, optimization, network analysis – to help address the 'hard' or computational aspects of particular types of problem. However, it has also broadened to include a range of 'softer' techniques to support the exploration and analysis of, for example, issues of corporate strategy. The ideas of messes and difficulties, hard and soft complexity, and hard and soft approaches to problem-solving, have all developed from this sort of work.

Job design and work organization

The recognition that people and the equipment they use form an integrated *socio-technical system*, and that attempts to improve performance therefore have to make sense in social as well as technical terms, was an early example of systems thinking in relation to problems of industrial management. Arguably, its insights are now taken for granted in management writing – although they are still easily overlooked in practice.

Computing and information systems

This area has spawned a wide variety of systems analysis and design methods, and now reaches as far as expert systems and knowledge engineering. Since informational and organizational processes are closely intertwined, the analysis of information use and requirements is no longer essentially, or even significantly, a matter of technical expertise in computing.

Systems design

This is another loose-knit family of methods, springing from classic engineering design, but now going well beyond specifically engineering contexts to areas such as the reorganization of production facilities and improved quality procedures or office processes. These methods usually combine general notions about what is required for particular sorts of system to work well with the systematic exploration and evaluation of options (usually by developing and examining a representation of the proposed system).

Accidents and failures

Ergonomics developed out of attempts to improve the design of equipment so that operators would be less uncomfortable, tired and error-prone. At about the same time, reliability engineering was being

---

developed to increase safety. The two fields came together in the search for ways of reducing and preventing a wide range of accidents and system failures – especially in large technological facilities where failure can mean catastrophe.

Game theory

This has provided a framework to analyse bargaining and conflict, and it has significant implications for negotiators and for competitive strategies.

Organizations as systems

In the 1960s the idea that organizations could usefully be understood as systems in particular environments had a pervasive influence on organization theory. The general idea was that organizations were better understood as *natural*, or adaptive, systems, rather than *rational*, or designed, systems.

Other disciplines, such as *information theory, engineering control theory* and *cybernetics*, have also influenced management thinking and practice through general concepts, models and analogies as well as through specific applications (for example, in relation to command and control systems for the armed services). More recently, *chaos theory* has found applications in economics and may, in due course, come to influence management thinking. In practice, these different areas are not separate and discrete; they have overlapped and exchanged ideas at various points.

Two sorts of people use systems ideas. Some simply want to get on with understanding their particular field of interest. They adopt and develop whichever ideas are useful to them and it is of no great significance to them that some of those ideas are used in a range of other contexts and form a loose-knit family. Other people, observing all these developments, have claimed that systems ideas and methods have important characteristics in common, not least a common philosophical base. For them, systems has emerged as an important field of interest in its own right. They are interested, in other words, not in particular sorts of systems but in systems *in general*.

The obvious question that arises is how much these different approaches actually have in common – beyond the use of the term 'system' and the extremely general notion of organized complexity. There clearly are differences, as has already been implied, but, despite the differences between them, people who make explicit use of systems ideas do share a set of common concerns or preoccupations. These underlying concerns about what is involved in comprehending and addressing complex problems, rather than the finer points of particular systems methods, are of most interest to managers. The rest of this session explains these underlying concerns and, in doing so, introduces ideas that will be used and developed at various points in the course.

The idea of a holistic approach

One aspect of a holistic approach is expressed by the maxim 'The whole is more than the sum of its parts.' In other words, we cannot understand the properties and functioning of complex entities simply by examining their constituent parts. Good players, to take the classic example, do not necessarily mean a successful team. Another aspect is the observation that plans and projects often fail because the people involved start with too narrow and simplistic a view of the situation (treating it more as a difficulty than a mess). A holistic approach, therefore, means trying to look at all aspects of an issue or a problem and trying to understand the context in which it is embedded, in terms of both its history and current external pressures and constraints.

The idea of a holistic approach is often contrasted with the reductionist methods through which science has progressed – that is, breaking things down and examining particular aspects, parts or relationships separately and in a controlled manner. This contrast reflects an important debate about the relationship between different *levels* of scientific understanding. Is biology reducible to chemistry and ultimately to physics? Is sociology reducible to psychology? It is now generally agreed that this is not the case: for example, the wing colour of a species of butterfly has to be compatible with the laws of physics and chemistry, but it is explained at the ecological level – by the evolution of predator–prey relationships. The moral for managers is that problems have to be addressed at the right level – most obviously, it is no use blaming *individuals* if their behaviour is simply the symptom of an *organizational* problem. This issue has already been alluded to in the discussion of levels of control in Session 1 (there will be more on this in the Organizations Block).

In practical terms, a holistic approach usually means first stepping back and generating a broader and rather more abstract view of the situation – rather than plunging straight into the details. This is not to suggest that details are unimportant – the point is to recognize *which* details are important. A holistic approach also tends to be an eclectic or interdisciplinary approach, gathering insights and considerations from a wide range of different perspectives. Various methods have been developed to assist in this process. They do not, of course, *guarantee* the broader and fuller understanding that is the aim of a holistic approach – only hindsight can assure you of that – but the aspiration expressed in the idea of a holistic approach can hardly be faulted.

QUESTION 3.3

Several members of staff are showing signs of stress and complaining of overload.

What would be (a) a reductionist and (b) a holistic approach to such a problem?

Multiple and mutual causation

In cases of organized complexity, what matters is the way the different aspects of the situation 'hang together' – the interrelationships and interactions between them. This means that the simple 'billiard ball' model of causality on which we were all brought up is distinctly unhelpful. By that I mean the simple, mechanistic idea of a causal chain in which A causes B and B causes C (and, moreover, the more of A, the more of B and the more of C). This model obviously has some application, but things are usually *far* more complicated. Such images of causality focus on particular events as the cause of other events, and ignore the many background conditions that have to hold if A really is to cause B. It will often be more helpful to think of B as arising from a peculiar combination of factors. Moreover, often the relationship will work *both ways*, with one factor both affecting and being affected by another. So, instead of looking for a simple chain of causation, it is more fruitful to look for *patterns* of causation which can account for the persistence or the transformation of particular practices and arrangements.

The example of performance-related pay in Session 1 illustrates these points. The thinking behind PRP is based on a view of motivation involving a very simple causal sequence. The reality of PRP, on the other hand, seems usually to involve very complicated causal processes in which many other factors are involved and casual loops play an important part – as Figure 1.9 tried to suggest. In general, organizations are continually evolving as those involved try to make sense of their changing situations and devise new plans or ways of coping. New schemes and procedures are introduced, but they may not work out in practice quite as intended; or they may have unintended consequences for others that generate further changes elsewhere. One thing leads to another and vicious, or sometimes virtuous, circles emerge. Too often people and organizations (that is to say, you and I) respond to failure by redoubling our efforts and by calling for more of the same. Such processes are obvious and familiar enough – at least we can recognize them in other people if not in ourselves. But they sit uneasily alongside those other views of organizations to which we also subscribe, such as the rational model considered in Session 1, with its view of organizations as the structured embodiment of elaborate error-correcting control systems. Recognizing the multiplicity of factors at work and the tendency for beliefs to be self-sealing suggests that error-correction will often be far more problematic. The study of failing organizations in particular shows that often those involved, like managers stuck in the 'fire-fighting' syndrome, have become trapped in ways of thinking and acting that they find utterly convincing – but which are demonstrably ineffective. These points have major implications for how individuals and organizations learn – or fail to learn – and will be developed as the course progresses.

QUESTION 3.4

What are the different factors that contribute to the 'fire-fighting' syndrome (as discussed in Session 2) and in what ways do different elements in the syndrome reinforce each other? To answer this question, draw a simple diagram in the style of Figure 1.9 using phrases such as 'actual workload', 'insufficient time spent on planning, preparation, delegation', 'need to spend time correcting/repeating earlier work', and link these phrases with arrows meaning 'contributes to'.

In what ways are a 'fire-fighting' manager's beliefs likely to be self-sealing? Try to add this element to the diagram.

(Spend up to 10 minutes on this exercise.)

Reframing issues

Problems are not just 'out there'; they are 'in here' as well. This was also illustrated in the discussion of time management, where it is often difficult to disentangle 'real' and self-imposed demands. How we think about a problem is a crucial element in the situation *but it is the hardest one for us to recognize.* Sir Geoffrey Vickers put it neatly when he said 'the trap is a function of the trapped' (Vickers, 1984). For example, a lobster pot is a trap for lobsters only because of the limitations of the understanding and behaviour of lobsters. By implication, 'management traps' are dangerous only because of the limitations of *what the managers involved usually recognize and value and do.* The trouble is that when we are trapped we tend to take our own state of mind for granted – which is partly why we are trapped.

So sometimes we need to be able to think our way out of problems, to be able to see the situation differently. Several different techniques for encouraging this are described by various systems and management writers, but the most general of them is simply the systems perspective and language itself.

A *system*, as we have seen, is simply a set of connected things or parts, an identifiable and complicated whole, a more or less discrete configuration of elements, activities, people, ideas, and so on. It is a familiar and very general term. It is closely, indeed logically, associated with two other terms: *environment* and *boundary*.

The environment of a system is comprised of those elements, activities, people, ideas, and so on that are not part of the system but which may, nevertheless, be important in understanding it. *System* is the foreground; *environment* is the background, the relevant context of the system. As for the term *boundary*, that is basically where the *system* ends and the *environment* begins.

Earlier, I distinguished messes from difficulties by their characteristic of being *unbounded* in important respects. Of course, if a problem is literally and completely unbounded, it extends to include 'Life, the Universe and Everything'. In practice, things are usually not that bad. Nevertheless, there is a genuine and important dilemma: on the one hand, one wants to avoid too limited and local an analysis; on the other hand, one really cannot rethink and change everything at once.

The language of systems does not solve this problem but it does provide a way of addressing it. The task is essentially to find a workable provisional boundary for the system containing the problem, or at least a significant part of the problem. But, in distinguishing between system and environment, one accepts that the problem is not self-contained, that it can be only partially disentangled from its broader context. Moreover, precisely because the term *system* is so general, and systems can be identified on many different bases, one can explore different perspectives and interpretations. Often, it will be a case of combining different views (rather than choosing between them), of progressively focusing on and detailing what seem to be the crucial aspects.

At this point it is important to understand that the term 'system' is being used in two rather different ways. First, there are *recognized systems* that can conveniently be thought of as existing 'out there'. Such systems are widely acknowledged, either because they are deliberately created (for example, a stock control system or a computer system) or because they are fairly discrete, naturally occurring phenomena that have long since been delineated and analysed by scientists (the nervous system and the solar system are examples) or just because they are popularly referred to as systems in a vague although useful way (the legal system and the economic system are examples). Secondly, there are *explanatory systems* whose status is more problematic. Indeed, if an explanatory system exists anywhere, it is in the mind of the individual who conceives it, for it is simply a particular way of thinking about selected aspects of the world and their interrelationships *which is useful in relation to the individual's concerns*. Systems of this second sort embody particular points of view and are only useful to the extent that they offer some insight into what is puzzling or troublesome.

As an example, consider the incineration problems (or were they opportunities?) of Nightingale General Hospital in Box 3.4. We can represent the different views of the problem as locating the incineration issues within different systems, or we can explore the relevance of different systems to the various problems. Are we simply talking about the *waste incineration system*? Or is it best understood as part of the hospital's *health and safety at work system*? Is incineration just one problem generated by a much broader *waste creation system*? And, if so, how can we minimize its impact? Or should we really be devising an entirely new money-making *waste services system* catering for several hospitals? Three of these possibilities are sketched out in Figures 3.5 to 3.7.

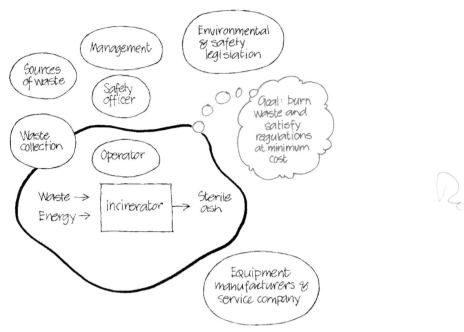

Figure 3.5   *Sketch of a waste incineration system*

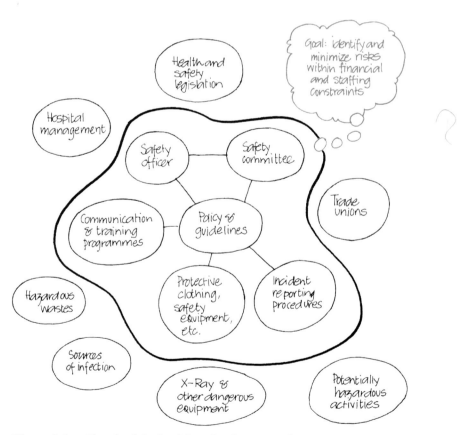

Figure 3.6   *Sketch of the health and safety at work system at Nightingale General Hospital*

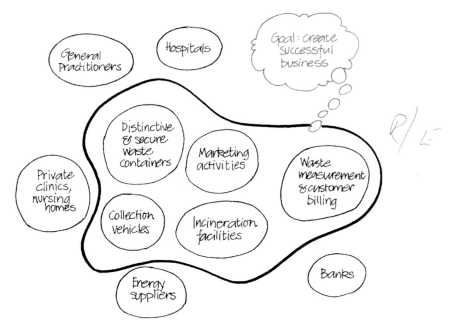

Figure 3.7   *Sketch of a waste services system*

So, each of these different viewpoints can be presented as involving a different sort of system, each with a different set of components and different goals. They are not all formal systems to which a hospital visitor could be directed; indeed, some of them cut across established departmental or organizational boundaries, highlighting an interconnected grouping of activities whose significance might not have been properly recognized before. Some of these explanatory systems are notional, tentative and exploratory; they are a way of representing a particular point of view.

There is nothing particularly clever, mysterious or taxing about this use of systems ideas. Indeed, it can be quite light-hearted: one well-tried and often revealing method of exploring a problem is to take some unsatisfactory aspect and view the situation as a system for producing that unwanted outcome. This was also illustrated in the Nightingale General case when the waste disposal problem was considered as the output of a *waste creation system*. Figure 3.8 begins to explore what such a system might look like.

Each of these figures and the systems they represent puts a quite different 'frame' around the nest of legal/incineration/cost/safety/waste issues at Nightingale General. None provides 'the answer' or captures 'the truth' about the situation. But they all highlight particular aspects and open up different options and lines of enquiry. Because we are all outside the situation, these different perspectives on the problem will seem rather obvious to you (as they do to me). You may be thinking, 'So what?'. But to the people closely involved in particular aspects of such issues, a range of possibilities will not be at all obvious – because, like you and me and the issues we are embroiled in, they have a particular, taken-for-granted view of what is *really* the problem.

So, this simple manœuvre of framing a messy problem in different ways, in terms of the different systems that may be relevant, is more useful than you might suppose.

That said, many people think intelligently about complex problems without ever mentioning the word 'system', and examining a problem in these terms is no *guarantee* of insight. All one can say is that the systems perspective and language provide a general framework within which many different views can

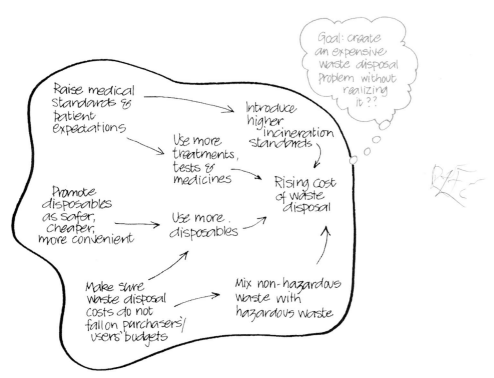

Figure 3.8   *Sketch of a system of activities to generate medical waste*

be made explicit, examined, developed, contrasted and, to some extent, combined.

In particular, it provides a way of exploring different boundaries for the problem and loosening the grip of one's preconceptions – which is why it has gained adherents.

QUESTION 3.5

Of the four systems referred to above and represented in Figures 3.5 to 3.8, which would be recognized systems and which would be explanatory systems?

Maps and models

I have referred several times to the importance of examining and exploring different views or aspects of messy problems. But we cannot examine most messy problems directly, nor can we observe and try out imagined new arrangements. All we can do is draw up some kind of map or model of the situation or of what is proposed and use that to think around and think through the possibilities and prospects. So, in working on complex problems, we need ways of piecing together and representing the complexity to ourselves in a way that allows us to scrutinize it and learn about it. Architectural plans, engineering drawings, a financial forecast on a spreadsheet, organization charts, diagrams of processes, charts of schedules and procedures – these are all *representations of complexity*. They are essential aids in addressing complex issues, not just in communicating finished proposals. By *externalizing* our thinking we can more easily examine it – and thereby discover where it needs to be revised or elaborated.

Hence, ways of mapping, modelling or otherwise representing complex situations – or, more precisely, of representing *our thinking about* complex situations – have been another recurring preoccupation of people interested in systems ideas and methods. They do not have a monopoly of interest in this area, of course, and many diagramming and modelling techniques are commonplace in management.

Because visual representations can be such powerful tools for managers, you have been provided with an array of materials to help you develop your diagramming skills. You will also be able to practise these skills at seminars, in your assignments, at the Residential School and during the remainder of your MBA. Many managers find it takes considerable practice before they become fully confident about using visual representation as an analytical tool or as an aid to creativity. You are therefore strongly recommended to read (or reread) the diagramming chapter in *The MBA Handbook*, look at the diagramming video 'Charting change' (Video-cassette 1, Section 3), and work through the diagramming workshop (Audio-cassette 4, Side 2). Do at least some of these now, aiming for familiarity with the main diagramming types (summarized in the index in Section 6 of the Course File) before submitting your first TMA. You will probably find it useful to revisit the materials before subsequent assignments and before the Residential School.

3.4 Conclusions

In Section 3.1, I offered the idea of roles as a way of reflecting on what influences how you behave in different situations. It is a way of integrating a functional, task-based view of what you are doing with more informal and intangible influences. It incorporates the personal, what we are bringing of ourselves to help us to be effective. It involves the recognition that we exist and work in relation to other people.

Appropriate action flows more easily when we feel we understand the role we are in. No action is certain, but the understanding of role is the individual's base for deciding by what authority he or she acts in relation to the organization's aims. Considering your role prevents a merely egocentric and undisciplined response to a situation, but it is not a set of rules or a fixed standard of behaviour. It is infinitely more flexible than that. It involves relating to the task of the organization, taking responsibility for that relationship and choosing an appropriate way of getting on with the work. It provides a basis for managing yourself.

This session also explored the idea that managers are essentially general problem-solvers who must deal with a never-ending stream of complicated issues as best they can. A consideration of the different sorts of complexity that managers face led, first, to a brisk overview of systems ideas in their various manifestations and, second, to a discussion of the recurring features of systems approaches to complex problems (context and breadth, patterns of causation, perspective relativity and modelling techniques).

The status of systems ideas, like so much else in management, is controversial. One view is that the emergence of the systems movement is intellectually very important and exciting. Systems provide an overarching and integrating philosophical framework that helps to combine different fields of knowledge. These fields become, in effect, special cases of a more general systems theory. Moreover, although necessarily abstract, the concepts and techniques that are being developed by people interested in systems ideas and their application to technological, managerial and policy issues are providing important new approaches and tools for real-world problem-solving.

The counter-view is that 'an approach' does not become any better, or even necessarily very different, by having the prefix 'systems'. It is not necessary to make much use of explicitly systems language – some writers and managers do, others do not. Moreover, the systems movement is in fact very diverse and includes people with very different ideas and assumptions. Having some words in common does not mean that they share a common philosophical framework. Far from becoming an integrating meta-discipline, systems is just one more esoteric discourse joining in the mutually confusing cross-talk of any technologically advanced society ...

You do not have to take sides. Indeed, arguments about the advantages and disadvantages of systems ideas can easily obscure the important general points about how we tackle problems involving organized complexity that this discussion has tried to highlight. You will return to these important topics later in your studies.

Objectives

After studying this session you should be able to:

- Define the term 'role', and give examples of the roles other people expect you to play in the course of your work.

- Analyse your own managerial activity in terms of Mintzberg's roles.

- Recognize, in case studies and from your own experience, examples of the following terms: 'role ambiguity', 'role conflict' and 'role negotiation'.

- Recognize, in case studies and from your own experience, elements of hard and soft complexity, and be able to explain briefly in your own words the different sorts of processes needed to address hard and soft problems.

- Define and use appropriately the following terms or distinctions: 'system', 'boundary', 'environment', 'difficulty'/'mess', 'recognized system'/ 'explanatory system', 'mutual causation' and 'multiple causation'.

- Draw simple diagrams to represent your thinking about a problem or situation and recognize occasions when such diagrams may be of value.

Contents

4.1 Introduction

Some of the early pioneers of management thinking believed that it was possible to discern 'one best way' of managing. The difficulties with this proposition soon became apparent and various contingency theories were developed – for example, theories of leadership and of organizational structure. These theories argued that what was best depended on the situation and they set out the sorts of factors that must be taken into account. So, for example, an appropriate leadership style has been shown to depend on the sort of task being undertaken, the power of the person leading, and the expectations of those being led; likewise, the most appropriate form of organizational structure has been shown to depend on such factors as size and the uncertainty associated with the organization's work and environment.

To begin with, the variety of different circumstances was fairly limited, and so the different ways of managing and organizing could be seen as variations on a theme. But as time has gone on the number of different factors to be taken into account has increased steadily and more and more different ways of managing have been identified – not least reported differences in the way men and women manage. This 'relativity' of management thinking – it all depends on who is managing what and where – raises difficult issues. It implies that there are many different sorts of management and many different ways of being an effective manager. How, then, can we judge what is 'good practice'? And will your 'good practice' work in our situation? For example, management as a body of thinking and teaching first flourished in the USA and, historically, the subject was concerned with the ways men ran large, privately owned, heavy-industry organizations. It is not obvious that such thinking will be equally appropriate for other people in other organizations in other countries.

Indeed, it is no longer obvious that we are talking about one and the same thing. It can be argued that the concept of management has become unhelpfully all-encompassing, that it is now based on purely abstract commonalities (like Fayol's functions of management, discussed in Session 1). In these extremely general terms management is rather obvious and unproblematic. Management only becomes interesting when the very different ways in which these functions can be discharged are considered. From this point of view, the important thing is to recognize and understand the different sorts of management that now exist – Japanese management, for example, or the management of public services. We simply mislead ourselves by thinking and talking of management in *generic* terms, because this approach neglects the all-important, specific, contextual differences in how management is actually done. What makes this issue particularly interesting and important is that, at the same time as more attention has been given to the *diversity* of management styles, practices and systems, management in a *generic* sense has been assigned greater and greater significance, and has been seen as relevant to a wider class of organizations – especially, but not only, in the UK. For example, huge efforts have been made on both sides of the Atlantic to identify generic management competences. So there is a running debate between two different tendencies. On the one hand, some people see management as involving a reasonably coherent body of ideas and practices and a core set of abilities that are relevant to all sorts of organizations, people and countries. On the other hand, there are people who see management as involving, in the huge variety of contexts in which the term can be applied, a highly disparate assortment of activities, systems and abilities *which are not all properly recognized and represented within management writing and teaching at the present time.*

Of course, we can quickly discard the extreme positions in this debate: no one is seriously going to argue that management practices in different situations, or management by men and by women, have *nothing* significant in common. Likewise, it is now widely recognized that the differences in management styles, roles and systems *are* significant and need to be understood. But this still leaves a considerable gap between the different positions. For example, is it important to recognize that certain 'essentials' of management are or should be the same everywhere? Or is this sort of claim a piece of unhelpful rhetoric, because the 'essentials' turn out to be so banal that the claim is empty or are contentious, making the claim doubtful and misleading?

As we shall see, this debate, like the debate about directive and empowering conceptions of management, is being played out in practice at the present time – so the issues have practical implications. For example:

- How can you tell whether a colleague, subordinate or partner in a collaborating organization is doing things *inappropriately* – or just doing things *differently*?

- Do we impose on others, or have imposed on us, models and assumptions about managing that are inappropriate?

- How much freedom should a foreign subsidiary have to do things differently?

- How appropriate and relevant will different ideas and practices discussed in this course be to your organization and situation – and how will you decide? What really can be learned from a case study based on events in a different country or industry?

Of course, there are no easy answers to these questions, and certainly none that I shall pass on to you. At this stage my purpose is to alert you to the significance of these issues and open up a debate that will continue throughout the course.

The aims of this session are to:

- Highlight the impact of national culture on organizations and management.

- Explore some of the ways in which the management task varies with differences in organizational purpose and size.

- Introduce the debate about gender differences in management.

4.2 Where you manage

We all know people do things differently in other countries – but do they do *management* differently? And do the differences make a difference, or are they merely rather quaint? After all, instructions are instructions, and the bottom line is the bottom line.

 In fact, the differences are substantial. They are described by Geert Hofstede in the article 'Cultural constraints in management theories' in *The New Management Reader*. This section is based on the article and you should read it now.

QUESTION 4.1

How do you imagine someone in France would view the notion of management as empowerment and the emphasis on team-work?

QUESTION 4.2

Hofstede argues not just that management differs around the world but that management theories reflect the countries in which they arise. How well does performance-related pay and the theory underpinning it fit in with his argument? What are the implications for the use of PRP?

ACTIVITY 4.1

Do you accept the characterizations of your culture given in the article? If you do not, is this because your organization is atypical or because the characterization is misleading?

Clearly, Hofstede's article raises major issues about the relativity of management theories, and these issues do not concern just cultural differences *between* countries. Most countries contain significant cultural minority groups within their boundaries which support their own organizations and business communities. Sensitivity to cultural differences is becoming important for all kinds of organizations, not just multinationals or those engaged in international trade.

4.3 What you manage (and what for)

Once upon a time, the world of organizations in the UK and countries like it was a relatively straightforward place. There were private companies, which might be large or small, and there were government agencies, which tended to be large. Figure 4.1 is a 'map' of such a world. Different sorts of organizations are located on the map according to the sorts of goals they pursue and their size (both affect management). For example, managerial roles tend to be broader and looser in smaller organizations, whereas larger organizations are more formalized, have more standardization and more specialization. With less control over their environments, managers in small firms are often more reactive, adaptive and opportunistic than those in larger firms – more concerned with tactics than longer-term strategies.

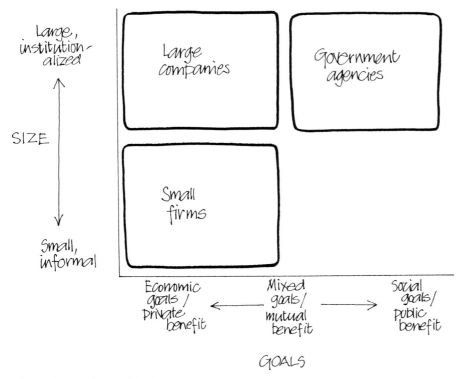

Figure 4.1   *The world of organizations, circa 1970*

Of course, there have always been other sorts of organizations: mutual societies and membership associations, for example, and charities and small partnerships of, say, doctors, conditioned by professional norms and values. But as regards organization and management, nobody paid them much attention; the attention was reserved for the large companies, which were interested in management writing, courses and research. The public agencies had their own body of thinking and practice: public administration.

The world of organizations looks very different now. I have tried to represent it in different ways in Figures 4.2 and 4.3 (overleaf). The large private organizations and the large public agencies are still there, but there are probably fewer of them. Both have been trying to reinvent themselves. The corporate bureaucracies have been broken up and flattened; they have become 'shamrock' organizations operating through networks of consultants, contractors and suppliers, or loosely-linked business units held together by a holding company. Indeed, it is not obvious where many should be placed on the 'map' in Figure 4.2: for example, a franchise operation of formally independent businesses is designed to combine economies of scale with the flexibility and commitment of small units, and would presumably straddle the central band of the map.

As for the right-hand side of the map in Figure 4.2, although some large public organizations remain – the armed forces, the central civil service – much has changed: public utilities have been privatized and now operate under regulatory supervision; ancillary services have been contracted out to small and medium-sized firms; and many of the mainstream public services are now being provided under contract by not-for-profit agencies. In other words, the organizations that provide these services have been reconstituted and their goals redefined in more commercial terms. Even where bodies remain formally part of the public sector, as with most hospitals in the UK, they now operate within quasi-markets, competing for contracts from the agencies who are responsible for purchasing services on behalf of patients and clients.

These trends have probably gone furthest in the UK but most European countries have experienced some of these changes. And some, like Italy, have had important small business and co-operative sectors for many years.

The potentially massive impact of e-business on the world of organizations is becoming very apparent.

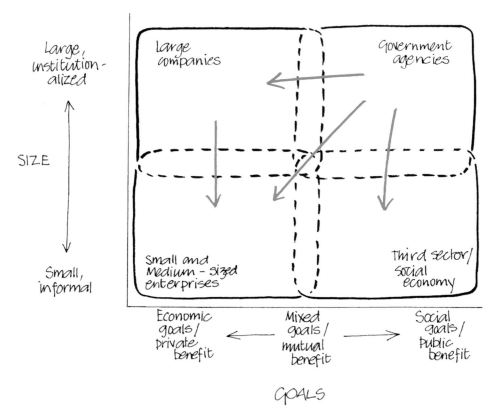

Figure 4.2   *The world of organizations now, highlighting the blurring of 'sectors'*

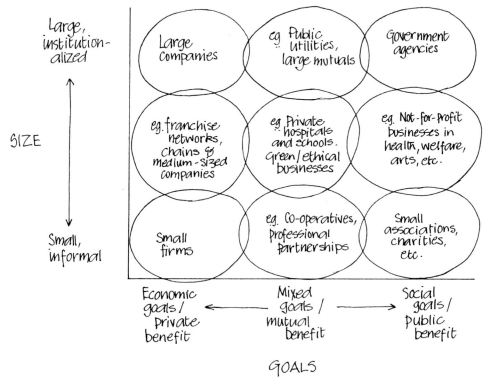

Figure 4.3   *The world of organizations now, highlighting the diversity*

ACTIVITY 4.2

Where on these maps would you locate your own organization? Where would it have been 20 years ago? Where do you expect it to be after another 20 years?

This way of thinking about the different sorts of organizations that produce or distribute goods and services has highlighted two points.

First, there is now a greater variety of organizational forms – or at any rate, far greater recognition is given to what may be called 'hybrids': organizations that are, in different ways, *between* the public and the private sectors, or those that are both large and small.

Second, management, as a body of ideas and practices, is now seen as relevant to – indeed vital for – all these organizations, not just the larger companies. Nevertheless, the question remains whether, and to what extent, management is different in these different sorts of organization, and especially between public and private organizations. One view is summarized in Box 4.1. The authors accept that private sector management has much to offer the public sector, but they argue strongly that private sector approaches are not enough.

In the UK there are now people with MBAs in a wide range of not-for-profit agencies, co-operatives and government departments. This would not have been true even 15 years ago.

Box 4.1   Stewart and Ranson on 'Management in the public domain'

John Stewart and Stewart Ranson argue that the private sector model of management reflects the purpose and conditions of the private sector. It is relevant to management in the public domain – although it has to be adapted if it is to be appropriate – but it is *not sufficient*. Important aspects of management in the public domain are distinctive and are not addressed within the private sector model. These include:

1   **Strategic management.** Governments and agencies can rarely opt out of particular services because costs and revenues are unfavourable or move into others because financial returns would be higher. Governments respond to market *failures* not market *opportunities*. They are guided by public values and aspirations collectively expressed, not by individual consumer (or taxpayer) choices. Some strategic management ideas (environmental review, the analysis of organizational strengths and weaknesses) can be readily adapted, but the public domain requires a different starting point. The competitive stance assumed by private sector strategic management is seldom meaningful.

2   **Marketing.** Thinking about marketing and customer relations can be a valuable stimulus in the public domain, but if used uncritically it distorts the public purpose. Public organizations are often concerned with need, rights and equity. They may have to assess, filter and discourage apparent demand, while facilitating access by those who are undemanding but more needy. Consumer demand is clear cut and measurable; social needs are ambiguous and contested.

3   **The budgetary process.** In the private sector, the budget is derived from a forecast of sales, and more sales generate more revenue. Budgets in the public domain represent political choices about taxation levels and allocations. The resources available do not necessarily, or even usually, increase just because demand for a service is greater than expected. For these and other reasons, financial

management in the public sector is different from that in the private sector.

4 **Public accountability.** The private sector model assumes accountability through market performance. Accountability in the public domain is more diffuse and demanding, not least because performance monitoring is often more difficult and 'value for money' hard to determine. Managers in public sector organizations have to be ready to explain and justify their actions to their political masters. They must be ready to respond to many voices, and the management process itself is often subject to challenge and debate. 'Open government', 'freedom of information' and the ombudsman have few parallels in the private sector model.

5 **Public demands and political process.** These are both conditions of the public domain. In the private sector, customer protest involves buying differently next time, and companies generally respond to this signal; but in the public domain, citizens can hardly move elsewhere and they have a right to be heard. They make up the public voice to which governments ultimately respond. Citizen action is not an interference in 'real' public management; it is part of the process by which public choices are made and values are expressed. It is essential for the legitimacy of management in the public domain.

In the light of such considerations, Stewart and Ranson distinguish between two models of management.

Private-sector model	Public-sector model
Individual choice in the market	Collective choice in the policy
Demand and price	Need for resources
Closure for private action	Openness for public action
The equity of the market	The equity of need
The search for market satisfaction	The search for justice
Customer sovereignty	Citizenship
Competition as the instrument of the market	Collective action as the instrument of the polity
Exit as the stimulus	Voice as the condition

These differences mean that the context and purposes of management are different in the public domain but they do not mean *all* management activity is different. As the authors point out, 'Letters are typed, vehicles are maintained and invoices checked in both sectors ... The immediate management of such activities may need to be little different in the public domain from the public sector'. Beyond this, however, management in the public domain becomes increasingly distinctive.

(Source: summarized from Stewart and Ranson, 1988)

QUESTION 4.3

(a) Within the UK the Open University Business School would generally be considered to be part of the public sector – even though, as part of The Open University, it is not directly controlled by government and earns most of its income from fees in a competitive marketplace. Is it better understood in terms of the private sector or the public sector model?

(b) If you managed the corporate affairs department of a large firm, which aspects of management in the public domain would be relevant to you?

'Corporate affairs' usually encompass internal communication of company policy, external (public) relations and corporate responsibility.

(c) What, in general terms, do you consider to be the strengths and the weaknesses of Stewart and Ranson's argument?

One difficulty with Stewart and Ranson's argument is that they seem to overlook the variety within both the private and public sectors. The private sector includes private nursing homes, farms, consulting firms, large manufacturing companies, public utilities and government contractors – and much else besides. Some of these organizations operate in competitive markets, others do not; some are highly regulated, others are not; some depend on government subsidies or contracts, others do not; some are international companies, others operate only nationally or locally. Likewise, some organizations in the public sector, which includes the armed forces, welfare agencies, universities, public utilities and hospitals, operate in competitive environments and depend on fee income, others do not; some are international organizations, others are not. One could envisage some being transferred to the private sector, but for others this makes little sense. Some are large organizations, some are small or networks of small organizations (such as the public library service in the UK). Some are governed by professional norms (social services organizations), others correspond more to the classic form of bureaucracies. Indeed, when the management of industries in both the public and private sectors are compared (for example, schools and leisure centres), the differences between the *industries* are more striking than the differences between the *sectors*. In other words, management is shaped more by the task – what the organization does – than by ownership or sector.

Another way of pinpointing the differences is in terms of the different *stakeholders* involved in organizations. Arguably, this explains many of the differences that concern Stewart and Ranson without the sweeping generalizations resulting from their heavy reliance on the public/private distinction. A stakeholder is a party with an interest in the decisions of an organization and the capacity to influence it. The principal stakeholders in a business and their relationships with the organization are shown in Figure 4.4.

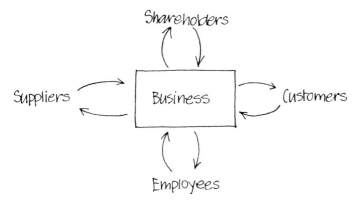

Figure 4.4   *The principal stakeholders in a business*

It is harder to draw the equivalent diagram for a government agency, but I have attempted it in Figure 4.5. Some of the stakeholders are the same but others have no obvious parallel with the business organization. Figure 4.6 shows the stakeholders and their relationship with a typical voluntary or not-for-profit organization. Two points are obvious about the patterns of stakeholder influence depicted in these diagrams: first, the different sorts of organization have different stakeholders; second, the nature of the relationships between stakeholders and organizations varies considerably – from the relatively clear-cut monetary exchanges that predominate in the case of businesses to more nebulous, but none the less important, exchanges in the case of public and not-for-profit organizations.

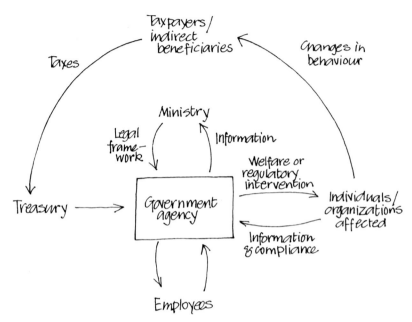

Figure 4.5   *The principal stakeholders in a government agency*

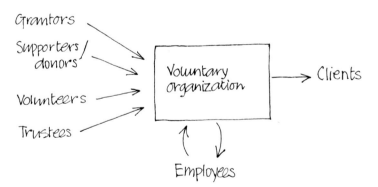

Figure 4.6   *The principal stakeholders in a typical voluntary organization*

The American management guru Peter Drucker has argued that US businesses could learn a great deal from their not-for-profit counterparts – particularly in the fields of organizational governance, staff development and motivation.

These diagrams are simplifications, of course, and they probably exaggerate the contrasts between the different sorts of organizations. For example, businesses also contract with other organizations which distribute the goods or services to the final customers; businesses, too, have to take account of the communities within which they operate and the wider publics who may one day be their customers; and regulatory bodies are important stakeholders in many businesses. Likewise, many not-for-profit organizations and government agencies charge fees for some of their services and have important relationships with suppliers. My point is simply that there are different sorts of stakeholders in organizations, having different relationships with those organizations. It is not part of the argument that those differences line up neatly into clear-cut distinctions between organizations in different sectors – quite the reverse, in fact.

Within this stakeholder perspective the commonalities and differences of management in different settings can be readily expressed. The management task varies because managers have to create and maintain relationships with very different sorts of stakeholders. On the other hand, what is common to management in all these situations is the need to deal with a range of stakeholders and to maintain a workable balance between them.

ACTIVITY 4.3

Draw a diagram of the main stakeholders in your organization. Then draw a diagram of the main stakeholders in that *part* of the organization for which you are responsible. How clear are your relationships with the different stakeholders? What difficulties are you aware of in balancing their competing claims?

Stakeholder analysis and the nature and extent of differences in management remain controversial topics. The arguments are not just, or even mainly, between those associated with private sector management (saying 'management is, or should be, pretty much the same everywhere') and those, like Stewart and Ranson, associated with public and not-for-profit management. Both these views are well represented within public and not-for-profit organizations. Likewise, stakeholder analysis is strongly contested within the private sector. Proponents of this perspective argue that companies must balance the competing claims of customers, shareholders, employees, suppliers, communities and the environment. They are no longer agencies of purely private purpose; they must recognize and accept their broader economic and social role and the public responsibilities this involves. Hence, although shareholders must receive a good return on their investment, the sole or overriding aim of a company should not be to enrich its shareholders. For today's companies this is a simplistic and confused aim (profit is an important measure of success, but not the only one, and not an end in itself); it does not provide the motivational basis for an effective, committed organization. Who can get excited by 'maximum medium-term earnings per share' as a mission?

The counter-argument is that stakeholder analysis is fundamentally muddled: it is wholly misleading to equate the different stakeholders when the nature of their involvement is so different. Of course, managers have to strike deals with customers, suppliers, employees and others – but only the shareholders have a literal *stake* in the business, one for which they paid, and one that is at risk. Moreover, businesses are undermined by being burdened with additional purposes and obligations. In an intensely competitive world they must be single-minded in pursuit of economic success – or there will be no company for the other (so-called) stakeholders to be involved in.

This debate is not heading for an early resolution – in different forms it can be traced back at least 200 years. The fact is that organizations define their purposes and values in different ways. But, in addition, important differences exist between countries in what are seen to be normal purposes and values. In Germany and other northern European countries, for example, the views of advocates of stakeholder analysis would not be controversial; whereas in the USA, the counter-arguments would be much more widely accepted. (There is more discussion of national culture in Book 11.)

4.4 Who is managing?

ACTIVITY 4.4

Spend no more than a minute answering each of the following questions – your immediate reactions and initial thoughts will be quite sufficient.

(a) What qualities do you associate with being a good manager? Write a list of seven (or more) qualities.

Leadership, Communication skills, Intelligence, Drive, Determination, Self-Belief

(b) Now write lists of the qualities you associate with men and with women.

All except 'leadership'

Compare your lists. Do the qualities you associate with good management have more in common with the qualities you associate with men or the qualities you associate with women?

You can see how your results from this exercise compare with those of other managers in the article 'Of stereotypes and differences: the debate about the ways women lead' by Donna Dickenson in *The New Management Reader*. This section is based on the article and you should read it now.

QUESTION 4.4

(a) Would you expect Elliott Jaques (see the *Managing Learning* course reader and Session 1) to favour a transactional or a transformational style of leadership?

(b) Rosener believes, on the basis of her interviews, that women lead in a different way from men. What grounds are there for challenging this interpretation of her evidence (and, hence, of challenging the way she conducted her study, compared with the design of the Greek study mentioned)?

(c) If the women in Rosener's sample really did lead in a different way from men what, in general terms, are the two different and competing explanations for this considered by Dickenson?

Celebrating difference can be liberating and empowering for women – they do not have to imitate men. However, Wacjman (1993) argued that it could also be a trap, because most men still did not value the different characteristics that women bring to organizations. In your experience, is this still the case?

Dickenson's article opens up a wide array of issues about the nature of gender differences in management, the extent to which such differences are the barriers to 'getting in and getting on' that women still face in many situations, and the difference it makes for organizations if a 'critical mass' of women (not just one or two) achieve management positions.

ACTIVITY 4.5

(a) Do your own observations bear out Rosener's view that women lead in a different way? Choose the three most senior women managers or colleagues you have worked with or for, think for a moment about their leadership style and give them a score of between 1 (very transactional) and 7 (very transformational).

Now choose three men in positions as comparable as possible to those of the women you have just considered and score them in the same way. What do you conclude?

(b) If you are a man, are you aware of having different expectations about the way women managers will behave, or about how you should relate to them? What are the differences, and on what are your expectations based?

If you are a woman, are you aware of having a strategy such as those reported by Laufer? What is it?

4.5 Conclusions

So where has this exploration of differences brought us? Three points stand out for me.

1   'Other' ways of management are no longer something strange and remote. The general trend is towards more interaction between different cultures, more hybrid organizations and public–private partnerships, and more women taking up senior management roles. There is now a blurring and interpenetration of national cultures, of different sectors and industries, and of traditional differences in the roles taken up by men and women. We must all come to terms with increasing diversity in the ways of managing and of being a manager.

2   The challenge lies in recognizing and working with differences, without creating or reinforcing stereotypes. The differences may be important in particular contexts but they are usually rather subtle. Sweeping generalizations concerning the nature and extent of differences can easily be as troublesome as overlooking the differences entirely.

3   The recognition of diversity is enriching management as a field. When we go abroad we learn about our own country. The similarities and the differences can both be surprising. It is precisely by encountering other ways of managing and of being a manager that we become aware of assumptions we have simply been taking for granted and learn about both the value and the limits of our own experience and ways of managing.

Objectives

After studying this session you should be able to:

- Explain briefly in your own words some of the main ways in which national culture can affect the way management is carried out, and the judgements we make about what is an appropriate way of managing.

- Explain briefly in your own words some of the ways in which the management task is affected by an organization's size, its purposes and the sorts of stakeholders it has.

- Summarize briefly in your own words some of the grounds for believing that ideas of appropriate management behaviour are not gender neutral.

- Critically appraise suggestions that women characteristically have rather different management styles from men, and the different explanations that may be offered for any such differences.

- Critically appraise arguments to the effect that management in a particular organizational setting is either just the same as or completely different from management in other organizations.

Contents

5.1 Introduction

The efficient and effective use of most of an organization's resources depends on the decisions, actions, and thoughts of its managers. The managers are resources that are as vital to organizational performance as its patented products and processes, capital or plant. Understanding the manager as a resource is a prerequisite to organizational improvement efforts whether the focus of these efforts is on strategy, structure, systems, culture or whatever.

(Boyatzis, 1982, p. 260)

During the 1980s the importance of developing effective managers was increasingly recognized. In the UK several reports (Constable and McCormick, 1987; Handy, 1987; Mangham and Silver, 1986) stressed that Britain's international competitive position was under severe attack, and that the country was in danger of losing out to foreign competition because its stock of managers was not adequately educated, trained and developed to meet the challenges of change and global turbulence. In order to guarantee its position within the world order and promote future growth and economic success, it was crucial that 'Britain do more to develop her managers and do it more systematically' (Handy, 1987, p. 15).

However, before companies and governments could do anything systematic to develop more and better managers they needed to be clear what they were talking about – and here is where the problems began. Mangham and Silver, for example, reported that when asked about management skills:

... many of the respondents provide replies in terms of functional skills at a level of abstraction that is of little value, and second, their vocabulary of skills is limited. Many, particularly of those doing little or no training of their managers, were unable or unwilling to specify the qualities, attributes and skills required of junior managers, for example.

(Mangham and Silver, 1986)

In fact, Mangham and Silver's respondents faced a real difficulty: everyone wants good managers, but what this really means is very difficult to express, or for that matter to agree about with others. 'What is clear is that there is no widely shared set of specific qualities, skills and attributes that will enable anyone to rate jobs or people, let alone create training programmes. The statements which find ready acceptance – communication, leadership, motivation – are too global to be of much use in selection or development' (Mangham and Silver, 1986). A major element in the drive to develop better managers has therefore been the attempt to generate frameworks for describing management attitudes, skills and behaviours within which those key attributes that characterize effective managers can be clearly identified.

At this point the concern for management development becomes intertwined with the broader trend towards *competence-based approaches* in education, training and development. This trend is international, although again it has been particularly noticeable in the UK, and where governments and employers have been concerned to increase the vocational relevance of the education and training done by schools and institutions of further and higher education. Competence-based approaches have four distinctive features:

- they concern the abilities and behaviours required to perform specified roles and tasks *to the standards required in employment*

- they focus on what staff and managers can do – their *behaviour and its outcomes* – rather than their experience and skills or the education they require

- they are concerned with *generic* work roles – that is, broad classes of jobs rather than particular positions

- they are *research-based* – aiming to replace arbitrariness and subjectivity with empirically validated and tested formulations.

Essentially, a management competence framework can be seen as a sophisticated person and job specification and form the basis of recruitment interviews, appraisal meetings, training needs analysis and/or reward systems.

This session explores the problems of identifying and defining management competences, compares different approaches to defining competence and considers the ways in which competence frameworks are used. You need to be able to understand the thinking behind competence-based approaches, and their limitations as well as their potential benefits, as they have become a key component in many aspects of human resource management.

A more immediate reason for a discussion of management competence frameworks is that they can provide templates for thinking about your own strengths and weaknesses as a manager, and about the priorities for your own development. In this way the discussion will prepare the ground for the final session of this book, in which we shall consider how management competences can be developed – and, hence, the ways in which you can use this course to develop yourself as a manager.

The aims of this session are to:

- Familiarize you with the debates about management competences and the uses to which competence frameworks are being put.

- Enable you to consider your own abilities as a manager and to identify areas of relative strength and weakness.

5.2 Approaches to specifying competence

This section briefly describes two contrasting approaches to the definition of management competences. These are interesting in their own right, but the contrast exposes the underlying research problems involved in trying to classify management skills and abilities in an accurate, reliable and useful manner.

Given the variety and complexity of management roles, and the lack of clarity and agreement already referred to, the task of developing a competence framework for managers and for management work was huge. Three basic approaches can be distinguished, focusing on:

- inputs – the desired qualities of the job-holder

or

- processes – the desired tasks and procedures to be carried out

or

- outcomes – the results desired.

Input models describe competence in terms of characteristics which competent (or sometimes outstanding) employees bring to the job. The first approach described below is an example of this approach and Table 5.1 (overleaf) shows relevant 'input qualities'. Note that measuring many of these qualities may be far from simple.

Process models describe what competent employees *do* in specific tasks and procedures. While these descriptions may be familiar, and easily recognized, they can be prescriptive, a disadvantage if an organization is changing rapidly and employees need to be flexible.

Outcome models describe competence in terms of results achieved by the job-holder. Arguably, these may be easiest to measure, but the indications for recruitment or development may be harder to perceive than for a process model. The second approach described below – the Management Charter Initiative – is phrased in process terms. However, much of what is assessed will inevitably be in the form of outputs.

A personal characteristics approach to management competence

This approach starts by trying to identify and define the distinguishing characteristics of excellent managers. It then relates these characteristics to the performance of different management functions. The seminal work that developed this approach – and indeed the whole idea of management competences – was done by Boyatzis (1982), who distinguished between 'threshold' competences (which all job-holders require) and 'differentiator' competences (which distinguish the outstanding manager from the average manager). He also distinguished between the different sorts of personal characteristics (skills, motives, social roles and traits) that contribute to particular competences.

The methodology involved is elaborate to say the least.

- It begins with an *analysis of measures of job performance* and of how that performance can be assessed.

- Next, *job element analysis* produces a list of weighted characteristics that an expert panel of senior managers perceives as important in distinguishing superior from average performers.

- The third step – *behavioural event interviewing* – involves individual discussions with current incumbents of the job (job performance data are also obtained for all interviewees).

- The interviewees' accounts are then coded for indicators of the specified characteristics and a *statistical analysis* establishes whether the thinking of the expert panel seems to be confirmed or requires refinement.

- The next step is to *identify or devise tests and measures of the competences* that have been painstakingly identified by the preceding steps.

- These tests, along with measures of job performance, are then *applied to a much larger sample of managers*, so that more elaborate statistical testing of the relationships between competences and performance, and between different competences, can be done.

Table 5.1 summarizes the management competences identified by Boyatzis using this method. It then goes on to relate these five 'competency clusters' to the tasks and functions performed by managers. (Competence and competency are synonymous.)

Table 5.1 Summary of Boyatzis' approach to management competences

Cluster	Competency
Goal and action	Logical thought (skill, social role)* Concern with impact (skill, motive) Diagnostic use of concepts (skill, social role) Efficiency orientation (skill, motive, social role) Proactivity (skill, social role)
Leadership	Logical thought (skill, social role)* Conceptualization (skill) Self-confidence (skill, social role) Use of oral presentations (skill, social role)
Human resource management	Accurate self-assessment (skill)* Managing group process (skill) Use of socialized power (skill, social role)
Directing subordinates	Positive regard (skill)* Developing others (skill, social role)* Spontaneity (skill)* Use of unilateral power (skill, social role)*
Focus on others	Perceptual objectivity (skill) Self-control (trait) Stamina and adaptability (trait)
Specialized knowledge	Specialized knowledge (social role)*

* Denotes a 'threshold competency'.

(Source: Boyatzis, 1982)

The MCI Management Standards: a functional approach

Functional analysis is the method of competence definition that has underpinned the process of establishing a national framework of competence-based vocational qualifications in the UK since the late 1980s. In the area of management, the body responsible for defining the standards for management qualifications has been the Management Charter Initiative – better known as the MCI. This was formed by major employers to raise the standards of management and is supported by the government.

On the basis of elaborate research and consultation processes with practising managers, functional analysis aims to identify the necessary roles, tasks and duties of the occupation rather than the skills of successful role incumbents. This yields an extensive list of elements of competence grouped under major functional or key role areas, with performance criteria developed to indicate minimum competence levels.

This procedure results in a highly detailed breakdown and specification of management performance that can be used by organizations for their own purposes but it also provides a framework against which managers in the UK can be assessed for a National (or Scottish) Vocational Qualification.

Table 5.2 shows the framework for a (UK) vocational qualification at Level 5 in Strategic Management. This is aimed at practising managers who have substantial and strategic responsibilities. (There are other levels of qualification for less senior managers, as well as a framework at Level 5 for operations managers.)

For the purposes of competence assessment, managers must be able to provide evidence of competence which meets the requirements of all the relevant criteria across the range of associated application areas.

Table 5.2   Strategic Management Level 5: key roles, units and elements of competence

Key purpose: To achieve the organization's objectives and continuously improve its performance

Key role	Unit		Element	
Key role A: Manage Activities	A6	Review external and internal operating environments	A6.1	Analyse your organization's external operating environment
			A6.2	Evaluate competitors and collaborators
			A6.3	Develop effective relationships with stakeholders
			A6.4	Review your organization's structures and systems
	A7	Establish strategies to guide the work of your organization	A7.1	Create a shared vision and mission to give purpose to your organization
			A7.2	Define values and policies to guide the work of your organization
			A7.3	Formulate objectives and strategies to guide your organization
			A7.4	Gain support for organizational strategies
	A8	Evaluate and improve organizational performance	A8.1	Develop measures and criteria to evaluate your organization's performance
			A8.2	Evaluate your organization's performance
			A8.3	Explain the causes of success and failure in organizational strategies
Key role B: Manage Resources	B5	Secure financial resources for your organization's plans	B5.1	Review the generation and allocation of financial resources
			B5.2	Evaluate proposals for expenditure
			B5.3	Obtain financial resources for your organization's activities
Key role C: Manage People	C3	Enhance your own performance	C3.1	Continuously develop your own knowledge and skills
			C3.2	Optimize your own resources to meet your objectives
	C6	Enhance productive working relationships	C6.1	Enhance the trust and support of colleagues
			C6.2	Enhance the trust and support of those to whom you report
			C6.3	Provide guidance on values at work
	C11	Develop management teams	C11.1	Assess the effectiveness of management teams
			C11.2	Improve the effectiveness of management teams
	C14	Delegate work to others	C14.1	Delegate responsibility and authority to others
			C14.2	Agree targets for delegated work
			C14.3	Provide advice and support for delegated work
			C14.4	Promote and protect delegated work and those who carry it out
Key role D: Manage Information	D3	Chair and participate in meetings	D3.1	Chair meetings
			D3.2	Participate in meetings
	D6	Use information to take critical decisions	D6.1	Obtain the information needed to take critical decisions
			D6.2	Analyse information for decision-making
			D6.3	Take critical decisions
			D6.4	Advise and inform others

(Source: Management Charter Initiative, 1997, pp. 4–5)

The MCI provides considerably more detail than is shown in the framework in Table 5.2, outlining very specific performance criteria to be met for each element, together with the knowledge requirements and evidence requirements. Examples of evidence are also given, to help managers seeking the qualifications. Box 5.1 shows them for Element C3.1 'Continuously develop your own knowledge and skills'.

Box 5.1   Performance criteria and range indicators for Element C3.1 Continuously develop your own knowledge and skills

Performance criteria

You must ensure that:

(a) you assess your performance and identify your development needs at appropriate intervals

(b) your **assessment** takes account of the skills you need to work effectively with other team members

(c) you prioritize your development needs so that they are consistent with your current objectives and the likely future requirements of your role

(d) your plans for personal development are consistent with the needs you have identified and the resources available

(e) your plans for personal development contain specific, measurable, realistic and challenging objectives

(f) you obtain support from **relevant people** to help you create learning opportunities

(g) you undertake development activities which are consistent with your plans for personal development

(h) you obtain feedback from **relevant people** and use it to enhance your performance in the future

(i) you update your plans for personal development at appropriate intervals.

Knowledge requirements

You need to know and understand:

Communication

- the importance of getting feedback from others on your performance and how to encourage, enable and use such feedback in a constructive manner.

Management competence

- the principal skills required for effective managerial performance
- the types of interpersonal skills required for effective team-work.

Organizational context

- the current and likely future requirements and standard within your job role and how they correspond to your level of competence as a manager
- appropriate people from whom to get feedback on your performance.

Training and development

- the importance of continuing self-development to managerial competence

---

- how to assess your own current level of competence
- criteria for prioritizing personal development needs
- how to develop a personal action plan for learning and self-development with realistic but challenging objectives
- the types of support which may be available from team members, colleagues, line managers and specialists
- how to identify the need for support, select an appropriate source and obtain required help
- the types of development activities and their relative advantages and disadvantages
- how to assess your personal progress and update your plans accordingly.

Evidence requirements

You must prove that you *continuously develop your own knowledge and skills* to the National Standard of competence.

To do this, you must provide evidence to convince your assessor that you consistently meet **all** the performance criteria.

Your evidence must be the result of real work activities undertaken by yourself. Evidence from simulated activities **is not** acceptable for this element.

You must show evidence that your **assessments** take account of
- work objectives
- personal objectives
- organizational policies and requirements.

You must also show evidence that you obtain support and feedback from at least **two** of the following types of **relevant people**:
- team members
- colleagues working at the same level as yourself
- higher-level managers or sponsors
- specialists.

You must, however, convince your assessor that you have the necessary knowledge, understanding and skills to be able to perform competently in respect of **all** types of **relevant people**, listed above.

Examples of evidence

Here are a few examples to give you some ideas about the sort of evidence you might be able to find in your daily work.

Work activities
- consulting relevant people
- reviewing your work with others.

Products or outcomes
- self-evaluation reports
- formal development plans
- personal profiles from self-assessment tools.

You may also provide short reports of your own, or statements from others who have observed your performance.

> *Written or spoken reports, describing*
> - how you identified your development needs
> - how you prioritized your development needs
> - how you matched your development plan to your needs
> - how you used other people to create development opportunities.
>
> *Witness testimony*
> - statements from people who gave you support and feedback.
>
> (Source: MCI, 1997, pp. 62–3)

You will see that the overwhelming focus of attention, as in any functional (or outcome) approach to competence is on observable behaviours, outcomes and performance. Competence is all about what an experienced manager can do – and can demonstrate that he or she can do – in relation to specific roles and functions; it is not directly concerned with what he or she has learned or how the competence has been developed.

In addition to relevant skills and knowledge, managers seeking a vocational qualification using the MCI framework need to demonstrate that they have the necessary *personal competences*. While these could be regarded as inputs, they are again assessed by observations of behaviour. The competences required will depend on the level of qualification sought and, indeed, different competences will be associated with each element of the framework. UK managers seeking an N/SVQ will be provided with full details. Table 5.3 (overleaf) shows the overall framework of personal competences for Level 5 in Strategic Management.

A comparison of the two approaches

Clearly, it would be easy to get lost in the finer points of both the Boyatzis and MCI frameworks. In this context, it is sufficient to emphasize two very general points.

First, even if the two approaches have much in common, they are also *very* different, and the term 'competence' comes to mean rather different things. The competence researchers' problem is depicted in Figure 5.1: they have to define and identify competence in terms of some selection and combination of capacities, dispositions, behaviours, outcomes and functions fulfilled – given that there is no one-to-one relationship between any of these (several dispositions may give rise to particular behaviours; several behaviours will, depending on the context, produce one or more outcomes, and so on) and *given that very many other factors also affect behaviour, outcomes and functions fulfilled.*

The personal characteristics approach focuses on capacities, dispositions and behaviour – and has the problem of showing that more or fewer of the identified characteristics really do account for differences in managerial performance. The functional approach largely avoids this problem. It defines competences in terms of results – that is, it concentrates on the goals, outcomes and behaviours end of the diagram – only the personal competency part of the framework addresses the personal attributes that contribute to performance.

The second important point is even more obvious: identifying management competences is not a straightforward exercise. Indeed, despite the enormous effort that went into developing the Boyatzis and MCI frameworks, they are open to a range of criticisms. Two, in particular, are worth noting.

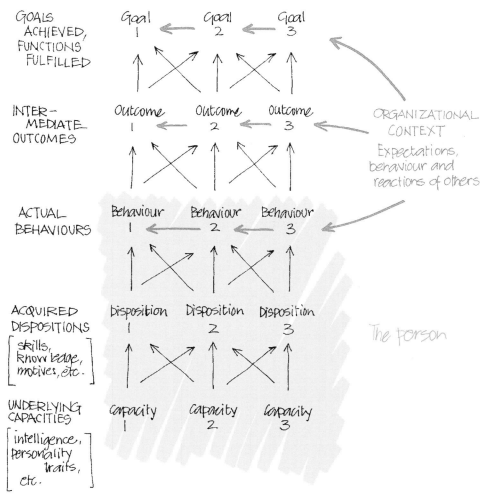

Figure 5.1   *The competence researchers' problem: which sorts of factors are to be called 'competences' – and with what justification?*

First, despite their apparent sophistication, both approaches are, in the end, *self-referential*. The complex research procedures by which the competences are defined and labelled depend heavily on the input of practising managers, and cannot avoid incorporating their assumptions about what constitutes 'good management'. We are dealing as much with *beliefs* about what contributes to effective management, and *beliefs* about who is a high performer, as we are with actual causes and effects – simply because the realities are incredibly difficult to establish. Perhaps the managers who display certain behaviours are the ones who tend to be rated as high performers – and then, not surprisingly, their behaviours appear to be associated with high performance.

Second, the frameworks have been criticized for being rather static and backward-looking. They define what it was to be competent in the past, not in the present – let alone the future. It is interesting to note, for example, that Boyatzis uses Fayol's classic view of management functions in his analysis. Likewise, the MCI's 'levels' are conceived of in terms of junior, middle and senior management – reflecting a rather traditional view of management in large, stable organizations with clear-cut chains of command and communication. Not surprisingly, managers in smaller organizations have complained that none really matches their experience. So, although these competence frameworks are designed to improve management in a fast-changing world, they may embody assumptions about organizational roles and relationships that can no longer be taken for granted.

Table 5.3   Framework of personal competences and associated behavioural indicators

Competency	Behavioural indicators
Acting assertively	Takes a leading role in initiating action and making decisions
	Takes personal responsibility for making things happen
	Takes control of situations and events
	Acts in an assured and unhesitating manner when faced with a challenge
	Says no to unreasonable requests
	States own position and views clearly in conflict situations
	Maintains beliefs, commitment and effort in spite of set-backs or opposition
Acting strategically	Displays an understanding of how the different parts of the organization and its environment fit together
	Works towards a clearly defined vision of the future
	Clearly relates goals and actions to the strategic aims of the organization
	Takes opportunities when they arise to achieve the longer-term aims or needs of the organization
Behaving ethically	Complies with legislation, industry regulation, professional and organizational codes
	Shows integrity and fairness in decision-making
	Sets objectives and creates cultures which are ethical
	Identifies the interests of stakeholders and their implications for the organization and individuals
	Clearly identifies and raises ethical concerns relevant to the organization
	Works towards the resolution of ethical dilemmas based on reasoned approaches
	Understands and resists personal pressures which encourage non-ethical behaviour
Building teams	*Managing others*
	Actively builds relationships with others
	Makes time available to support others
	Encourages and stimulates others to make the best use of their abilities
	Provides feedback designed to improve people's future performance
	Shows respect for the views and actions of others
	Shows sensitivity to the needs and feelings of others
	Uses power and authority in a fair and equitable manner
	Relating to others
	Keeps others informed about plans and progress
	Clearly identifies what is required of others
	Invites others to contribute to planning and organizing work
	Sets objectives which are both achievable and challenging
	Checks individuals' commitment to a specific course of action
	Uses a variety of techniques to promote morale and productivity
	Identifies and resolves causes of conflict or resistance
	Communicates a vision which generates excitement, enthusiasm and commitment
Communicating	Listens actively, asks questions, clarifies points and rephrases others' statements to check mutual understanding
	Identifies the information needs of listeners
	Adopts communication styles appropriate to listeners and situations, including selecting an appropriate time and place
	Confirms listeners' understanding through questioning and interpretation of non-verbal signals
	Encourages listeners to ask questions or rephrase statements to clarify their understanding
	Modifies communication in response to feedback from listeners

Focusing on results	*Planning and prioritizing*
	Maintains a focus on objectives
	Tackles problems and takes advantage of opportunities as they arise
	Prioritizes objectives and schedules work to make best use of time and resources
	Sets objectives in uncertain and complex situations
	Focuses personal attention on specific details that are critical to the success of a key event
	Striving for excellence
	Establishes and communicates high expectations of performance, including setting an example to others
	Sets goals that are demanding of self and others
	Monitors quality of work and progress against plans
	Continually strives to identify and minimize barriers to excellence
Influencing others	Develops and uses contacts to trade information, and obtain support and resources
	Presents oneself positively to others
	Creates and prepares strategies for influencing others
	Uses a variety of means to influence others
	Understands the culture of the organization and acts to work within it or influence it
Managing self	*Controlling emotions and stress*
	Accepts personal comments or criticism without becoming defensive
	Remains calm in difficult or uncertain situations
	Handles others' emotions without becoming personally involved in them
	Managing personal learning and development
	Takes responsibility for meeting own learning and development needs
	Seeks feedback on performance to identify strengths and weaknesses
	Changes behaviour where needed as a result of feedback
	Reflects systematically on own performance and modifies behaviour accordingly
	Develops self to meet the demands of changing situations
	Transfers learning from one situation to another
Searching for information	Establishes information networks to search for and gather relevant information
	Actively encourages the free exchange of information
	Makes best use of existing sources of information
	Seeks information from multiple sources
	Challenges the validity and reliability of sources of information
	Pushes for concrete information in an ambiguous situation
Thinking and taking decisions	*Analysing*
	Breaks processes down into tasks and activities
	Identifies implications, consequences or causal relationships in a situation
	Conceptualizing
	Uses own experience and evidence from others to identify problems and understand situations
	Identifies patterns or meaning from events and data which are not obviously related
	Builds a total and valid picture from restricted or incomplete data
	Taking decisions
	Produces a variety of solutions before taking a decision
	Balances intuition with logic in decision-making
	Reconciles and makes use of a variety of perspectives when making sense of a situation
	Produces own ideas from experience and practice
	Takes decisions which are realistic for the situation
	Focuses on facts, problems and solutions when handling an emotional situation
	Takes decisions in uncertain situations or based on restricted information when necessary

(Source: adapted from Management Charter Initiative, 1997, pp. 118–121)

Indeed, there is some concern about the extent to which one *can* generalize about what constitutes 'competent' management, given the wide range of organizations in which managers perform very different roles in the face of very different expectations. How could a description of desirable attributes or actual work tasks be broad enough or flexible enough to capture the varied and ever-changing nature of the role?

These criticisms and difficulties point to limitations in the work that has been done, but they do not mean that these and other competence frameworks are worthless or misleading. Indeed, the development and use of competence frameworks within large organizations is trying to overcome these limitations – as we shall see in the next section.

QUESTION 5.1

(a) What doubts about the Boyatzis model might reasonably be expressed by (i) a manager from a different culture area and (ii) women managers? If they were justified, what might be the implications of such reservations?

(b) What doubts might Kanter (see Box 1.2) have about the MCI framework in Table 5.3?

ACTIVITY 5.1

It might be useful to do a rough-and-ready audit of both your current abilities and the requirements of your current job using one of the frameworks discussed in this section.

Try using one or both of them to think about what you do and about your capabilities as a manager. For each element of competence you need to consider how important it is in your job now and will be in the future; and to what extent it is already an area of competence for you or, alternatively, something that you suspect you need to develop further. If you are not sure about your levels of competence in particular, how might you find out? You might also consider whether there are aspects of your work that are not adequately captured in the framework you are using.

You could usefully spend 20 minutes on this exercise. As well as sharpening your thinking about your development priorities, it will make the discussion in the next section more meaningful.

5.3 Competences in action

This work is summarized in the article by Sparrow and Bognanno in the *Managing Learning* course reader.

So much for the general idea of competence frameworks. But how are they being used in practice? The general answer is that they are being used in recruiting and selecting managers, in performance management and human resource planning, and in change management and 'culture building' in organizations.

However, the use of competence frameworks in diagnosing development needs and in career planning is of most immediate interest at this point. Therefore, you should now read the article by Tony Cockerill, 'The kind of competence for rapid change', in the *Managing Learning* course reader.

QUESTION 5.2

In what terms – using those provided in Figure 5.1 – are Cockerill's
high-performance competences defined?

QUESTION 5.3

What are the main similarities and differences between the 11 high-
performance competences listed on page 73 of the article and Boyatzis'
competences listed in Section 5.2 of this book?

QUESTION 5.4

What are the three ways in which Cockerill says managers can use knowledge
of their own strengths and weaknesses?

QUESTION 5.5

In what ways, according to Cockerill, are the self-ratings you did in
Activity 5.1 likely to be inaccurate – and do you agree?

Cockerill's discussion reinforces several points made earlier – in particular, the
difficulty of apparently sophisticated research being self-referential. But the
discussion of the use of competence frameworks, and the fact that considerable
effort and expertise are required to be able to rate people accurately against
these frameworks, presents a realistic picture of the current state of the art.
Bear in mind, however, that Cockerill, Sparrow and Bognanno are all
practitioners and advocates of the use of competence frameworks. You are
entitled to remain sceptical of their grander claims for 'behavioural engineering'
and to wonder what other people might say about the work reported.

5.4 Conclusions

Although there are both practical problems and academic objections to
drawing up a comprehensive list of management competences, considerable
progress has been made. It remains unclear how reliably and objectively
competences have been defined; the extent to which competences are generic is
problematic; and the existence of rival frameworks developed for different
purposes and contexts means that there is still no common language. On the
other hand, the discussion of management skills and abilities is now far more
sophisticated than it used to be. 'Is this chap officer material?' may be a joke
now but it is not so long ago that staff selection and development decisions
were made on the basis of such vagaries and implicit stereotypes. Moreover, the
existence of many different competence frameworks should not obscure the fact
that they generally have quite a bit in common – certain themes recur.

Indeed, the consideration of management competences has brought together
several of the different ideas about what management involves discussed in
this book.

- The functional view of management has provided one way of defining
  management competences.

- The debate between what I loosely call the directive and the empowering views of management has reappeared in rival frameworks.

- The importance of managers not being trapped in reactivity, which was emphasized in the discussion of Mintzberg and of time management, is endorsed by many competence frameworks.

- Luthans' findings about the behaviour of effective managers are echoed in the concern for various aspects of people management and communication that recur in the different frameworks.

- The importance given to concept formation and use, and to various aspects of information-gathering and the analysis of that information in decision-making, fits in with the view of management as primarily a matter of problem-solving.

The next question is how, and how far, can management competences be developed through your work on this course?

Objectives

After studying this session you should be able to:

- Explain briefly to other people in your organization the reasons why management competences have become a focus of interest, what competence-based approaches have in common, and the sorts of uses to which they are put.

- Distinguish between different definitions and usages of the idea of management competences.

- Contribute to discussions about the strengths and weaknesses of particular competence frameworks in human resource management in your organization.

- Appraise yourself using a competence framework, recognizing the difficulties and limitations of such an exercise.

THE LEARNING OF MANAGEMENT

Contents

6.1 Introduction

You will have already have grasped, from *Starting Your MBA*, that studying B800 will significantly affect the way you think about your job and your organization. What, and how much, you will learn from this course will depend on many things.

ACTIVITY 6.1

Spend a minute listing as many factors as you can that may affect the sorts of things different managers will gain from their study of, and involvement with, this course. Imagine that in a few months' time a member of your tutorial group, or even yourself, feels *trapped* because they are not learning anything worth while from the course. Why might that be?

The sorts of factors that come readily to mind are: the amount of time that a manager can spend on study; how well the members of a tutorial group work together; the extent to which the course materials are relevant to the challenges and demands at work; and how familiar the material covered is (although whether some familiarity means a manager will learn more, less or differently is another matter). If you have encountered the idea of 'learning styles', you may well have included on your list the 'fit' between the way the learning has been designed and an individual's preferred way of learning.

Learning styles are discussed in several of the readings in the *Managing Learning* course reader.

All these are important, but one crucial factor is missing from the list, although not, I hope, from *your* list. The notion of someone feeling *trapped* was designed to prompt the recognition – and recall – of an important point. Session 3 argued that 'the trap is a function of the trapped'; when we face problems, we tend to take our own state of mind for granted. In the context of this course, how you think about and approach the learning it offers can have important consequences for what you learn from it. To start considering the sorts of expectations that may be involved, and how important those expectations can be, you should now read part of 'Why managers won't learn' by Graeme Salaman and Jim Butler in the *Managing Learning* course reader. Read the sections 'How and why managers learn' and 'Resistance to learning' on pages 36 to 39 and then attempt Question 6.1.

QUESTION 6.1

(a) Salaman and Butler's description of the assumptions made by trainers about what managers want, and the form taken by their management courses in consequence, echo some characteristics of managerial behaviour discussed earlier in this book. What are they?

(b) If these orientations to learning actually prevent certain sorts of learning, why might some managers and management trainers still hold them?

My own view is that Salaman and Butler's criticisms of management training are a bit too harsh and sweeping (as in most fields of activity, I suspect the quality and benefits vary widely). Nevertheless, I think they have correctly identified some characteristic traits of management training, and they are also correct in arguing that these traits, while popular with participants, also restrict the sorts of learning that can take place. Their argument serves as a warning: it suggests that one way to learn not very much is to approach the course in terms of its immediate relevance – in effect, scanning through it for the bits that can be readily applied in your current work. The trouble is that to appear relevant in this way, these bits must not challenge other aspects of your thinking and practice, and they must fit in with your current judgements about what is realistic in your (current) organization. But how can such an approach ever help you recognize and overcome the limitations of your existing way of thinking? A manager with this approach will learn some things, of course – but only as long as they do not involve thinking differently about anything significant.

So what is the alternative? And is all this just intellectual footwork to justify a traditional approach to university teaching, with an emphasis on absorbing abstract theory and principles? Far from it. Indeed, the fairly widespread assumption that it will be that sort of academic course provides *another* self-defeating way of approaching the learning that is available. Such an orientation leads to compartmentalization: there is much sophisticated thinking around and about management ideas in one part of managers' lives; while in another part they go on pondering their day-to-day problems and work relationships in just the same terms they always did.

What the Salaman and Butler article highlights is both the importance and the difficulties attached to the notion of relevance. Managers are *bound* to make judgements about what is relevant in terms of the appropriateness and *acceptability* of ideas given the organizational contexts in which they work. In Salaman and Butler's words: 'They would be mad, and soon redundant, if they did anything else.' So judgements about relevance are essential, but they are crucially tied up with the ways in which managers 'read' their current situation and they may also be influenced by restrictive assumptions about what a 'good' idea looks like (neat, self-contained, giving clear implications for action, and so on). These judgements and assumptions are exactly what one can expect will change if a manager becomes more discerning through participating in such a course.

So how does such learning happen, and how does it relate to the idea of management competences discussed in Session 5? In fact, a course like this offers several different types of learning, some more immediate and tangible than others. Moreover, as with the discussion of competences, how people learn to manage is relevant to you in two ways – for your own benefit and for the benefit of other people.

The aims of this session are to:

- Explain how the course works, so that you approach it with realistic expectations and can decide how to make the most of it, given your circumstances and your existing skills, knowledge and understanding.

- Present models of learning that will be relevant to you as a manager with responsibility for the learning and development of other people, as well as to your own learning.

The session starts by considering management as a subject, albeit rather a strange one, and considers how absorbing this subject can contribute to your competence as a manager. The limitations of this view lead to a different perspective – that of management as a personalized practice that each of us develops. Between them, these two perspectives should clarify the different sorts of learning that are usually involved and indicate what you can and cannot expect from this course – using some of the material that you have already studied in this book to illustrate various points.

6.2 Absorbing the subject

The conventional idea of a subject is a 'body of knowledge' – comprising theories, well-founded generalizations and principles, techniques and methods – that is learned and then applied in appropriate situations. So, if management is a subject, what is the knowledge, and where does it come from?

In the most general terms the subject has emerged and developed through the recognition of particular recurring problems and the devising of 'recipes' of one sort or another for dealing with them – approaches, techniques, ways of analysing or thinking about the situation. Initially, of course, this was done in terms of particular functions (accounting, marketing, production management, and so on) and has been 'fed' by the application of ideas from several academic disciplines – but many general and cross-functional recipes have also been developed (strategic management, quality management, and so on). So, looked at this way, the subject of management provides answers to a huge and ever-expanding array of questions. How do you manage a low-performing member of staff? How do you introduce a new information system? How can you make sure the new product is ready in time for the Christmas market? ... In addition, though, some more general, overarching frameworks have been developed that encompass particular families of concepts, techniques and approaches – for example, scientific management, or the human relations school, or the systems ideas briefly introduced in Session 3.

So the subject of management is a loose-knit and sprawling assortment of doctrines, principles, techniques, ideas and guidelines. In addition, *un*like most other academic subjects, management is also a burgeoning popular literature, prominently displayed in, for example, airport bookshops. From Fayol to John Harvey-Jones, the reflections of successful managers have become best-sellers. Legions of management consultants and industrial journalists offer their ideas – ranging from justifiably influential books, such as Peters and Waterman's *In Search of Excellence*, to fairy stories and exhortations.

In Search of Excellence (1982) was an important book but it was methodologically flawed. Many of its 'best-run companies' were in difficulties a few years later.

As a body of knowledge, management is a peculiar and diverse field. Certainly, the management literature does draw on and incorporate the concepts and findings of established academic disciplines such as *economics*, *psychology* and *organizational theory*. But it would be misleading to suggest that this is typical.

Much management theory is simply a development of certain familiar, general metaphors derived from, for example:

- engineering – the organization as a machine (hence, control mechanisms, sensors, feedback, and so on)

- biology – the organization as an organism adapting to its environment

- government – the organization as an arena for the pursuit of interests, the struggle for resources and the exercise of power.

All these metaphors make a contribution. Each is a useful half-truth, illuminating some aspects of management and obscuring others. The point is that the solid research base of management as a subject is limited – especially when the pace of change and the diversity of management are taken into account. In any case, as the example of performance-related pay illustrates, even when considerable research has been done, the scholars may still not agree on the results or their conclusions may be unwelcome for other reasons.

There are other difficulties with the notion that management is a body of principles and techniques that can be learned and then applied. The messy problems we face as managers do not come ready-labelled. Hence, deciding what the issues are is half the problem. Are the pressures you are under signs of poor time management? Or are the pressures symptomatic of a much broader problem of policy and structure in your organization? Clearly, how you 'read' the situation is crucial in deciding what sort of problem you are dealing with, and in deciding about the often-conflicting advice available.

The fact that there are few certainties in management does not mean that the subject has nothing to offer. It means that its offerings have to be critically appraised, selected and adapted (this is not unusual at postgraduate level). With this important qualification, the idea that learning involves absorbing the subject of management has some validity. Thus, this course introduces a broad array of what are generally felt to be the central ideas and 'recipes'; but it also tries to indicate their limitations as well as their value. These central ideas and recipes are very varied – some are 'hard' and quantitative, others 'soft' and qualitative – and they involve very different sorts of learning. Some involve the sorts of skills that develop through practice and feedback, and you may already have some of these in considerable measure. Others involve analytical techniques taught through structured exercises. Yet others involve becoming proficient in the use of a new terminology or style of discourse, and this really happens only by trying it out in discussion and interaction with other people.

An understanding and use of new management concepts can affect management behaviour – when we think about a person or situation differently, we relate to that person or situation differently. A broader repertoire of frameworks, models and ideas increases one's discrimination and ability to diagnose situations. All the typologies of management competence discussed in Session 5 acknowledged the importance of, and incorporated, diagnostic, analytical and conceptual skills. Through having available a much wider range of management ideas one becomes more discriminating and takes account of a broader range of factors.

Nevertheless, this traditional view of learning – one that sees management as a subject to be absorbed – has some serious limitations. Learning the concepts can affect behaviour – *but it may not*. I have already mentioned the problem of compartmentalizing – of keeping one's thinking about management ideas separate from one's thinking about actual management issues. Likewise, Sparrow and Bognanno referred to the distinction between 'representational

For example, if it is a time management problem, does it show that you should lower your standards – good enough is good, after all? Should you delegate more – or would that be adding to someone else's time management problem? How do you decide which prescriptions to follow, which views to adopt?

learning (i.e. new words, language and symbols) as opposed to behavioural learning (i.e. sustained change in what people actually do)'.

More generally, this is the problem of 'management-speak': knowing all the jargon and currently fashionable words but using them only in the most general terms. This practice avoids the challenge of relating the ideas to the messy realities of actual management – which is usually much more difficult (reality never quite fits). If the ideas are not brought down to earth and used to think in practical terms about specific aspects of a situation, they will not provide a new angle or insight; they will simply remain at the level of rhetoric, and at best be used to dress up in fashionable attire what one believed in all along.

A second problem with the idea of management as a subject that is taught and absorbed is even more fundamental: it overlooks all the learning that happens in other ways, especially through everyday experience, when we are not specifically trying to learn. This brings us to another useful way of thinking about management learning.

QUESTION 6.2

(a) List briefly, in your own words, at least three limitations of the notion that management is a body of ideas, principles and techniques that can be absorbed and applied.

(b) What judgements are involved in taking a principle and applying it? (Are such judgements part of the subject of management?)

6.3 Learning through management practice

Another, powerful view of management learning starts, not with management as a subject, but with management as a personal practice that each of us is engaged in at work on a daily basis – and one that we are learning all the time.

In *Starting Your MBA* you were introduced to Kolb and Fry's (1975) model of the process by which people generate from their experience the concepts, rules and principles that guide their behaviour in new situations, and then modify them to improve their effectiveness. It is a process that is both active and reflective, concrete and abstract. In its most generalized form, the process is usually represented as the four-stage cycle shown in Figure 6.1.

Learning can start anywhere in the cycle. 'Learning the subject' focuses on the abstract concepts and generalizations. So this view of learning actually incorporates the traditional view presented in Section 6.2 as well.

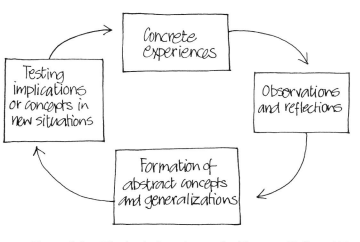

Figure 6.1   *The basic learning cycle (Source: Kolb and Fry, 1975)*

This experience-based learning process applies to all aspects of our learning – our general personal and social development, formal training and education, as well as our more specific professional and work-based learning. In practice, your work-based management learning – your experience of learning 'on the job' – will be made up of several factors, including:

- reflecting on your own immediate practice

- drawing on the 'recipes' of procedures, systems, routines, and so on that already shape the work you are required to do

- learning from the guidance and advice of other people – you are 'shown how' by bosses, peers and subordinates

- observing positive and negative role models – we try to imitate those who seem effective at particular activities, and vow that we will do everything we can not to make the mistakes of those whose failings we have to suffer.

Taking account of these factors, it is helpful to draw up a modified version of the learning process which reflects the cycle of action, feedback and error correction by which our repertoire of ideas, skills, recipes, and so on is gradually elaborated (Figure 6.2).

From the basic idea of the learning cycle different learning styles can be identified. Chapter 8 of *The MBA Handbook* develops this idea. Use it to identify styles you might need to develop and the activities to help you do this.

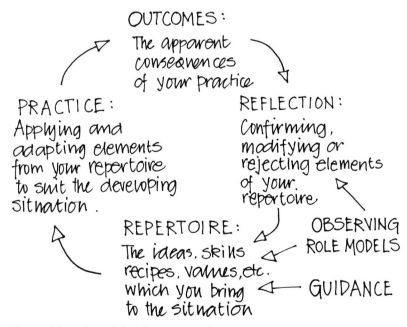

Figure 6.2   *A modified learning cycle*

The simple cycle in Figure 6.2 can gradually build up an elaborate and discriminating repertoire that allows the experienced manager to recognize quickly what is required, anticipate problems and economize on time and effort. What is more significant is the fact that important aspects of this accumulating 'experience' will be extremely hard to convey to others – *competent people know far more than they can express*. When competence involves really complex judgements – as in the case of management – it is only with the greatest of difficulty, if at all, that competent people can explain what they know and do.

Clearly, therefore, practice and experience are absolutely central to the process of management learning. First, broadly defined professional competence – made up of skills, abilities, ideas, recipes, values, and so on – cannot readily be taught; it is not the sort of thing we can just explain.

Secondly, it is through practice and experience that 'knowing about' becomes 'knowing how', that common sense becomes elaborated and more discerning, and our inappropriate behaviours come to be modified or abandoned.

Although experiential learning is fundamental to management development, it does suffer from several significant limitations. There are two basic problems.

First, the learning process may not happen, or it may generate inappropriate learning. This can occur because:

- the very characteristics of managerial work – its pace and pressure, the variety, brevity and fragmentation of activities, and so on – inhibit reflection on practice and, hence, the completion of the learning cycle

- we may learn the 'wrong' lessons, preferring, for example, to blame other people for difficulties and overlook inappropriate aspects of our own behaviour

- the guidance and advice we receive, and our available role models, may have many shortcomings and weaknesses.

Secondly, experience may be very restricting and limiting – consistent success in one sort of situation can actually make it very difficult to adjust to different situations. Sometimes we have to un-learn what we have become good at to cope with a new job. Moreover, there is more to learning than what is directly available and accessible to individual experience. How, for example, can you learn the basics of marketing by experience if your role involves no marketing activities and little contact with marketing staff? Without attention to the range and nature of the external context and inputs, the learning cycle can become closed and self-reinforcing rather than developmental.

'A manager's job is characterized by pace, interruptions, brevity, variety and fragmentation of activities' (Mintzberg, 1980)

ACTIVITY 6.2

How important have the following different ways of 'learning by experience' been for you?

	Rarely	Sometimes	Frequently
Explicit guidance and advice:			
from superiors	❑	❑	❑
from peers	❑	❑	❑
from subordinates	❑	❑	❑
Copying someone who seemed effective	❑	❑	❑
Trying to avoid someone else's mistakes	❑	❑	❑
Gradually working out a recipe through the learning cycle	❑	❑	❑

Which of the suggested limitations of learning by experience apply in your case?

The potential limitations of learning by experience point to ways in which a course like this can contribute to your professional development. It is neither an alternative to nor a substitute for the learning cycle of day-to-day experience – it is intended to feed it and make it work better and faster. The following points apply to the OUBS MBA programme as a whole and not just this course.

1   This course provides a structure and a discipline which should allow you to pause, reflect on what you have been doing and how you have been doing it, and think through the issues.

2   This course assists reflection on practice by providing frameworks and ideas, some of which will give you a fresh understanding of problems you have experienced – a new 'angle' on them – so that you can respond to them in a different way. By extending your understanding it triggers new progressions through the learning cycle.

3   This course is a way of finding out about unfamiliar skills, techniques or procedures, so that you can start cultivating them. This leaves a great deal for you to do, but at least it avoids 'reinventing the wheel' and gives you access to what has worked in other organizations.

4   The course materials provide a library of concepts and techniques which you can refer back to in the future when a new job introduces different challenges. Some parts are bound to be more immediately relevant than others, but knowing what other management ideas are available when you need them should enhance your capabilities.

5   The different sorts of activities and assignments provide a safe setting in which to experiment with some of the new ideas and techniques or to practise and improve some of your 'recipes'.

6   Through tutorials and the like this course provides opportunities to share experiences, encounter different attitudes and perspectives, and learn from other managers.

So, your experience and your study are complementary. However, this depends on you making the effort to relate the materials to your own work experience (Figure 6.3).

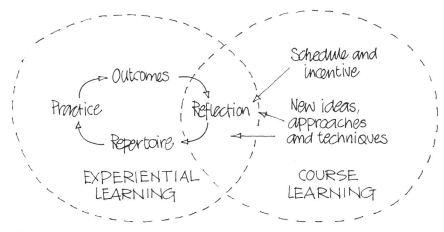

Figure 6.3   *The integration of study and practice*

QUESTION 6.3

From your work on this book so far, give specific examples of points 1 to 3 from the list above.

6.4   Review and conclusions

In this session it has become clear that management as a subject and management as practice are complementary. Learning is affected by a variety of factors, including our own individual styles and preferences and the environments in which we manage.

The variety of teaching and learning methods used in this course are there to help you engage in the full learning cycle. The conceptual frameworks offered will make your reflection more productive. Management is a complex, diverse and rapidly changing field. Organizations require clear thinking, not clichés and trendy ideas. Managers therefore need a broad grounding in the basic disciplines of management and a range of interpersonal and other skills. They also need reflective skills, the ability to stand back from each situation, recognize assumptions and judgements they are making, continually test these against evolving experience, and develop their own conceptual frameworks throughout their working life.

Objectives

After studying this session you should be able to:

* Critically appraise the idea that management is a body of knowledge comparable with other academic subjects.

* Identify, using examples from your own experience, the contributions to and the limitations of (a) course-based learning and (b) practical experience in the development of management skills and practices.

* Set goals for your own management learning and plan the measures needed to achieve them, anticipating and avoiding some of the common pitfalls.

QUESTION 1.1

Inconsistency between different objectives would mean different parts of the organization were working at cross-purposes and risked undermining each other. Or there might be an unnecessary duplication of effort. Inconsistency between different *levels* of purpose would show itself in actions that achieved immediate targets at the expense of longer-term goals or vice versa. I very much doubt that inconsistency can always be avoided: some tension between different objectives, and between the short and long term, is virtually inescapable. Balancing and combining conflicting objectives is an important part of management.

QUESTION 1.2

The boss may have no clear goals for the organization; he or she may not be receiving accurate information about what is or is not being achieved; he or she may not understand the work or how it is done (for example, efforts to improve performance may make no difference, or may even make things worse).

QUESTION 1.3

The key differences are in the much greater attention Snow *et al.* give to *lateral* relations (brokerage) as opposed to the vertical relationships (direction, monitoring, and so on) that receive most attention in the traditional view. They also emphasize external linkages as opposed to internal relationships. Organizations are being disassembled into smaller linked units, and the design, operation and caretaking of networks have become key management activities. But just as Fayol acknowledged the need for lateral contact (co-ordination), Snow *et al.* would presumably recognize that – within particular small units – vertical relationships, supervision, and so on will still have a place.

QUESTION 1.4

(a) People are employed as individuals in hierarchies in which other individuals – managers – are held accountable for their work and performance. That accountability and authority are necessary for competitive effectiveness in an organization.

(b) I noted the following reasons: hierarchy has been mistaken for autocratic management; Japanese forms of management have been misunderstood; success has been built on accountability rather than on democratic groups and teams; and it has been wrongly assumed that information technology would change the basis of management.

(c) The main concern for Jaques is to define the correct (or requisite) number of layers of management and the correct authority associated with each level; he sees empowerment as reflecting a more general and misguided concern for 'less layers and power down'. Fostering networking between staff undermines the essential duty of managers to mediate between subordinates in a constructive, humane way.

(d) Jaques would argue that it is only through the establishment of the requisite structures and managerial leadership and authority that each individual has the fullest opportunity to use his or her potential to the fullest. He sees this as 'one of the hallmarks of a truly democratic free enterprise society'.

(e) The centrality of individual contracts and accountability, rather than non-accountable groups; achieving the requisite structure; defining lateral working relationships more clearly in terms of accountability; filling management roles with people of 'the right calibre'; and taking steps to revise managerial leadership practices.

QUESTION 2.1

(a) When the time and effort spent on working out the 'best' decision would be better spent on attending to other, more important, matters. Or, more precisely, when the additional benefits to the organization resulting from a 'very good decision', as against one that is 'good enough', are not as great as the benefits that would be obtained by giving more time and attention to other matters.

(b) Bounded rationality is an appropriate strategy when the decisions appear to be relatively unimportant, or when many other matters need attention. The effort involved in approximating to the rational model may be justified when a decision is likely to have far-reaching consequences, and those consequences can be estimated and evaluated (more or less). However, other factors will also be important – for example, in order to command support and acceptance, it may be important that a decision is *seen* to be made in a rational way.

QUESTION 2.2

The careful and systematic nature of the study and the very large number of managers observed lend credibility to the results. (The findings are also consistent with some other research – for example, that organizational visibility is a powerful predictor of who will get promoted.) However, it is doubtful whether any implications can be drawn for particular managers, in relation to either their own conduct or that of their subordinates. The relationships between activities and success and effectiveness were not analysed on the basis of different industries or functions or levels of management. The findings may also now be out of date: the research was done before the rapid changes of the 1980s and 1990s. In the new 'network organizations' different patterns of behaviour may be required both for success and for effectiveness. So one cannot tell in any particular situation whether, for example, more networking might actually contribute to *greater* effectiveness and more people management *reduce* effectiveness. Overall, I believe Luthans' research has demonstrated that the conceptual distinction between effective and successful managers needs to be taken seriously, but how this distinction applies in particular circumstances is not at all obvious.

QUESTION 2.3

The answer to this question is given by the three ways of using time ineffectively: the 'fire-fighting' syndrome, the poor judgement that often accompanies being stressed, and the failure to distinguish between the urgent and the important.

QUESTION 2.4

Time management ideas involve: (a) planning; (b) the attempt to make optimal use of available time, choosing between alternatives on a rational basis (using priorities as criteria); and (c) continual monitoring and control so that activities can be adjusted in the light of progress and changing circumstances.

QUESTION 3.1

The manager may be relating to subordinates in an inappropriately 'parental' way – because this is the only way of being 'in authority' that the person observed as a child. Indeed, a directive and punitive approach is probably the surest way of bringing out the 'inner child of the past' in subordinates.

QUESTION 3.2

(a) Unless the betting agent suspects that he or she may be the target for some kind of betting 'coup', this is a matter of hard complexity. The agent's aim is to set odds that will attract enough bets on different horses to ensure that, whichever one wins, there will be more than enough cash to pay the punters who backed the winner. So, if one horse is being heavily backed, reducing its odds will make other horses relatively more attractive to punters. Betting agents become adept at handling the calculations and judgements that are required (or they go out of business).

(b) Historical records and documents are incomplete, often contradict each other, and are certainly open to different interpretations. This is definitely a matter of soft complexity.

(c) Mainly hard complexity: there may be some complications associated with interpretation – for example, trends in different sorts of accidents – but this is essentially a matter of calculating the relative frequency and costs of different sorts of claims and deciding on a scale of premiums.

(d) Mainly hard complexity: it concerns costs, reliability, effectiveness and the like. Some soft complexity might be involved in relation to the aesthetic value of the different designs.

(e) Mainly soft complexity: even quantitative data on traffic trends are likely to be controversial. Different interests and perspectives are bound to be involved. No doubt someone will wonder whether a bridge is even necessary or whether two small bridges is a better idea.

QUESTION 3.3

The reductionist approach would locate the problem in the individuals, and responses might include training, counselling or moving the staff. A holistic approach would consider developments within the department and wider organization which might be contributing to the stress experienced by the individuals. It might address the problem at organizational and departmental levels – as well as at the individual level.

QUESTION 3.4

My answer is shown in Figure A (overleaf) but the diagram could be drawn in many other ways (using different phrases, including greater detail, and so on). It is, of course, a simplification, but it captures the main ideas.

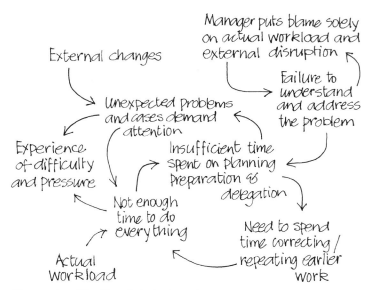

Figure A *The 'fire-fighting' syndrome*

In the diagram three factors combine to create the 'fire-fighting' syndrome: the actual workload, the real unpredictability of some matters, and a failure to understand the syndrome. The relative importance of these factors can vary greatly, and will be difficult to determine. The scope for explaining the difficulties by reference to only the first two factors can give rise to a self-sealing belief about what is happening.

QUESTION 3.5

The incineration system and the safety-at-work system are both recognized systems. Of course, some people might talk about the incineration facility and staff, or about safety policy and procedures, rather than use the term *system*. But they would quickly recognize what someone who referred to these as systems had in mind. By the same token, the hospital waste creation system is clearly an *explanatory* system. If you mentioned this during a management meeting you would almost certainly be challenged about what you meant by it and, even if you were not challenged, it is not clear whether the other people would have the same configuration of elements in mind.

I think the waste services system can be argued either way: clearly, it is a notional, possible system in the situation described – which suggests it is *explanatory*; on the other hand, the general idea of a specialist commercial service disposing of hazardous waste is readily grasped, so to that extent one could argue that this is just a particular sort of business system, and business systems are very familiar.

QUESTION 4.1

Since maintaining a social distance between superior and subordinates is important in French culture, the emphasis on team-work and empowerment might well be problematic. One manager – formerly with Michelin – who commented on a draft of this book, answered this question as follows: 'With alarm, as it might challenge the essentially bureaucratic structure of French society and management'. He went on to say that team-work would be accepted as long as it was not a threat to the *système*. But another manager thought the article contained too many caricatures and stereotypes that no longer applied. This issue is actually discussed on Video-cassette 1.

QUESTION 4.2

Performance-related pay seems to fit well as an illustration of Hofstede's argument: it focuses on individual performance and thus assumes an individualist orientation, and it has received by far the greatest prominence in the USA. The implications are that PRP stands a better chance of working in the USA than in many other countries.

QUESTION 4.3

The point of (a) and (b) is to highlight the way in which features of the two models can appear in organizations that are supposedly of the other sort. This is very obvious in the case of the Open University Business School – ostensibly in the public domain, but most of the features of the private sector model apply in considerable measure. Less obviously, managing the corporate affairs department of a large company may well be like management in the public domain. The day-to-day work involves negotiating the organization's commitments and policies on various matters of wide concern and communicating these to various internal and external constituencies. Moreover, the department does not earn any income itself (indeed, it has to bid for resources, just as government ministries have to bid to the Treasury for resources).

Opinions can reasonably differ on the answer to (c). My own answer is as follows. The strength of Stewart and Ranson's argument is that it highlights many areas of difference – in relation to strategy, relationships with customers, the place of values, budgetary processes, and so on – while still accepting the relevance of many management practices that have developed within business organizations. On the other hand, I find the contrast between the public domain and the private sector model rather simplistic. This point is developed further in the text.

QUESTION 4.4

(a) This is not straightforward! I think it is too easy to say that Jaques would favour a transactional style. In principle, I think he would have no objection to a transformational style as long as the underlying authority relationships were not confused. On the other hand, I have a lurking doubt about whether *in practice* Jaques would recognize transformational leadership as a valid use of a manager's authority.

(b) The main problem is that Dickenson's research was based on *self-reporting* by her respondents. So all we know for sure is that male and female managers *describe* what they do in different terms. Whether they *really* lead differently is not at all clear, for the reasons Dickenson gives in discussing the Greek study. This methodological weakness is important because it is *common* in management research. It is vital, therefore, to be able to cast a critical eye over the methods used in studies that report new findings about management.

(c) One explanation is that they lead differently because of innate or learned differences between men and women. The other explanation is that they lead differently because of the sort of leadership required in the kinds of dynamic, non-traditional, medium-sized organizations in which they work and have been able to advance (and so, by implication, in a more traditional organization, women might come to display more transactional styles of leadership). These two explanations could both have some validity and are not necessarily incompatible.

QUESTION 5.1

(a) The general issue is whether the same factors would have emerged from the research if it had been done in another culture area and/or among women managers (or, at least, a gender-balanced group of managers). This is the issue of such research being self-referential. More specifically: (i) some of the competences – for example, concern with impact, use of unilateral power – suggest that the Boyatzis framework endorses behaviour that would be culturally problematic in less indivdualistic cultures; and (ii) the number of women managers has increased considerably in the USA and the UK in the 20 or more years since Boyatzis did the research (he seems not to have considered the possibility that there could be different ways of being a competent manager). If such doubts are well founded, using Boyatzis' framework in management recruitment and management development would disadvantage managers from other cultures and women managers.

(b) The general problem here is that the skills Kanter believes are now demanded of managers do not come across clearly within the MCI competence framework. Lateral relationships and team-work are mentioned but hierarchical relationships receive far more attention. Also, the focus is on relationships within the organization; negotiating and networking externally receive little recognition.

QUESTION 5.2

The competences are defined largely in terms of behaviours, although some use is also made of intermediate outcomes (for example, 'creates a positive climate') and dispositions (for example, 'wants to do things better').

QUESTION 5.3

The main similarities are that many of the ideas are common to both lists: proactivity, self-confidence, impact, presentation, the formation and use of concepts. However, the high-performance list is defined more behaviourally, and is not predicated on hierarchical relationships (although, to be fair to Boyatzis, the 'directing subordinates' cluster are threshold rather than differentiator competences).

QUESTION 5.4

They can learn to make better use of their strengths, especially by recognizing new contexts in which to deploy them; they can learn to compensate for their weaknesses through collaboration with colleagues who are more competent in the relevant areas; and they can develop greater competence in one or two of the areas in which they are currently weak.

QUESTION 5.5

According to Cockerill, your ratings were probably lenient and undifferentiated. However, some people, particularly some women, tend to rate themselves severely – that is, they underestimate their capacities.

QUESTION 6.1

(a) For me they are reminiscent of Mintzberg's discussion of the skilful superficiality that managers develop, the fragmentation and variety they become used to, and their preference for live contact and action. Perhaps, too, the emphasis on prescription (and certainty) in the training echoes the idea of the decisive manager pretending that the uncertainty surrounding his or her work is non-existent.

(b) This approach to learning is likely to work initially, when managers first become exposed, in lively and enjoyable ways, to certain simple but important ideas which clarify and affirm what the managers were doing anyway. As a result, managers and management trainers can point to evidence that the approach works, and so the assumptions about what a good idea looks like and how learning happens may become a self-sealing system of belief. The fact that certain other sorts of learning become extremely difficult within this set of assumptions will be invisible to the managers, and perhaps also to the trainers. In other words, this is another area in which effectiveness is very difficult to determine.

QUESTION 6.2

(a) (i) The solid research base is very limited, and many principles are contested or are based only on impressions and anecdotes.

(ii) As a subject, management contains a wide range of often-contradictory implications and prescriptions.

(iii) Practices are widespread for reasons that have little, if anything, to do with their efficacy (for example, PRP).

(iv) The subject may be 'learned' without it affecting behaviour to any great extent.

(v) The rate of change and the diversity in management situations mean it is unclear how far what works in one circumstance will work in another.

(b) This involves at least three judgements: deciding what sort of issue one is facing; choosing a principle or an approach that is appropriate and acceptable; and deciding how best to apply or adapt that principle or approach to the circumstances. These judgements do not fit easily with the idea of a body of knowledge and they are not usually an explicit part of the subject. Nevertheless, developing the capacity to make these judgements is obviously essential and needs to be seen as integral to 'absorbing the subject' – as it would be in other forms of professional education (which face the same issue).

QUESTION 6.3

The different categories in this question are not very distinct, and of course I do not know which ideas in the course worked for you. But one answer might be as follows.

1   You probably spent some time thinking about your role as a manager.

2   This book includes several broad frameworks that you might have found useful in understanding aspects of your practice – for example, the directive and empowering views of management. You might also have found particular ideas useful – for example, the distinction between hard and soft complexity, or between effective and successful managers.

3   You may have decided to try some of the time management ideas.

REFERENCES

Boyatzis, R.E. (1982) *The Competent Manager: A Model for Effective Performance*, John Wiley and Sons Ltd, New York.

Constable, J. and McCormick, R. (1987) *The Making of British Managers*, BIM and CBI, London.

Deci, E.L. and Ryan, R. (1985) *Intrinsic Motivation and Self-Determination in Human Behaviour*, Plenum Press, London.

Eden, C., Jones, S. and Sims, D. (1983) 'Misunderstandings', in Paton, R. (ed.) *Organizations: Cases, Issues, Concepts*, Harper and Row Publishers in association with The Open University, London.

Freedman, J.L., Cunningham, J.A. and Krismer, K. (1992) 'Inferred values and the reverse-incentive effect in induced compliance', *Journal of Personality and Social Psychology*, Vol. 62, No. 3, pp. 357–68.

Gordon, T. (1977) *Leadership Effectiveness Training*, Wyden Books, New York.

Handy, C. (1987) *The Making of British Managers: A Report on Management Education, Training and Development in the USA, West Germany, France, Japan and the UK*, National Economic Development Office, London.

Handy, C. (1991) *The Age of Unreason* (3rd edn), Arrow Business Books Limited, London.

Institute of Manpower Studies (1993) *Pay and Performance: The Employee Experience*, Institute of Manpower Studies, London.

Kanter, R.M. (1989) 'The new managerial work', *Harvard Business Review*, November–December, pp. 85–92.

Kohn, A. (1993) 'Why incentive plans cannot work', *Harvard Business Review*, September–October, pp. 54–63.

Kolb, D.A. and Fry, R. (1975) 'Towards an applied theory of experiential learning', in Cooper, C.L. (ed.) *Theories of Group Processes*, John Wiley and Sons Ltd, New York.

Management Charter Initiative (1997) *Management Standards. Strategic Management Level 5*, MCI, London.

Mangham, I.L. and Silver, M.S. (1986) *Management Training: Context and Practice*, sponsored by the ESRC and the DTI, University of Bath School of Management, © June 1986 University of Bath School of Management.

Mintzberg, H. (1980) *The Nature of Managerial Work*, Prentice Hall, Englewood Cliffs, New Jersey.

Peters, T.J. and Waterman, R.H. (1982) *In Search of Excellence*, Harper and Row, New York.

Pugh, D.S. and Hickson, D.J. (1989) *Writers on Organizations* (4th edn), Penguin Books, Harmondsworth.

Sisson, K. and Storey, J. (2000) *The Realities of Human Resource Management*, Buckingham, Open University Press.

Stewart, G.B. (1993) 'Rethinking rewards', *Harvard Business Review*, November–December, pp. 37–8.

Stewart, J. and Ranson, S. (1988) 'Management in the public domain', *Public Money and Management*, Vol. 8, Nos 1 and 2, Spring/Summer, pp. 13–19.

Vickers, G. (1984) *The Vickers Papers* (edited by Open Systems Group), Harper and Row, London.

Wacjman, J. (1993) *Organizations, Gender and Power: Papers from an IRRU Workshop*, Warwick Papers in Industrial Relations, No. 48, December, University of Warwick Industrial Relations Research Unit.

Williams, R.S. (1998) *Performance Management*, International Thomson, London.

ACKNOWLEDGEMENTS

Grateful acknowledgement is made to the following sources for permission to reproduce material in this book.

Text

Pugh, D.S. and Hickson, D.J. *Writers on Organizations*, Penguin Books, 1971, fourth edition 1989. Copyright © D.S. Pugh, D.J. Hickson and C.R. Hinings, 1964, 1971, 1983. Copyright © D.S. Pugh and D.J. Hickson, 1989. Reproduced by permission of Penguin Books Ltd; *Box 5.1:* Management Charter Initiative (1997) *Management Standards. Strategic Management Level 5*, © Crown Copyright. Reproduced with the permission of the Controller of Her Majesty's Stationery Office.

Figures

Figure 6.1: Kolb, D.A. and Fry, R. (1975) 'Towards an applied theory of experiential learning', in Cooper, C.L. (ed.) *Theories of Group Processes*, John Wiley and Sons Ltd. Reprinted by permission of John Wiley and Sons Ltd.

Table

Table 5.1: Boyatzis, R.E. (1982) *The Competent Manager*. Copyright © 1982 John Wiley and Sons Inc. Reprinted by permission of John Wiley and Sons Inc.; *Table 5.2:* Management Charter Initiative (1997) *Management Standards. Strategic Management Level 5*, © Crown Copyright. Reproduced with the permission of the Controller of Her Majesty's Stationery Office; *Table 5.3:* Management Charter Initiative (1997) *Management Standards. Strategic Management Level 5*, © Crown Copyright. Reproduced with the permission of the Controller of Her Majesty's Stationery Office.

Cover

Images Colour Library.